To Ru

Best wishes

Julia Clements

MY LIFE WITH FLOWERS

MY LIFE WITH FLOWERS

Julia Clements

CASSELL

Cassell Publishers Limited
Villiers House, 41/47 Strand
London WC2N 5JE

First published 1993

British Library Cataloguing in Publication Data
A catalogue record for this book is available
from the British Library

ISBN 0–304–34246–7

Distributed in the United States by
Sterling Publishing Co. Inc.
387 Park Avenue South, New York, NY 10016–8810

Distributed in Australia by
Capricorn Link (Australia) Pty Ltd
PO Box 665, Lane Cove, NSW 2066

Set in Monophoto Palatino by
August Filmsetting, Haydock, St Helens
Printed in Great Britain by Hartnolls Ltd

Contents

Illustrations

ACKNOWLEDGMENTS

I would like to express my grateful thanks to:

the late Theo A Stephens who first gave me a chance;

Bill and Marta Annett for their encouragement;

C Clark Ramsay of Newnes Pearson publicity department, who helped me and my subject to get off the ground;

all those kind members of NAFAS who have constantly urged me to write of my experiences;

Francis Bennett, formerly of Thomson Books, who told me I must write of my start;

June Mayhew, my faithful secretary, who typed the first draft of this book;

Ann Rowen MBE, who has waded through all my bad typing and made it presentable;

Iris Webb for her generous Foreword;

members of flower clubs all over the world who have given me a platform and

Thelma Nye for her loyal support and never-failing belief in me and my purpose in writing this book.

Finally, as my journeys have been undertaken over a period of time, although my facts and figures were correct at the times of my visits, changes in officers in organizations worldwide may mean that I have omitted many names and places from this book. So many people have done Trojan work to consolidate that which was started so long ago and my thanks go to them also.

The author and publishers would like to thank those flower arrangement societies, individuals and photographers who have so kindly supplied illustrations for this book.

Foreword

This is an age when people such as entrepreneurs, oil prospectors and technicians, fly the world daily on urgent lucrative business. Julia Clements, however, is unique in her journeying from East to West without administrative support and with no financial gain in sight. She goes solely by invitation. Those who hope for her visit seek only her inspiration, artistic skills and knowledge about which they have heard or read. Their hope is that she will pass on these qualities to them.

So, armed only with long cardboard boxes, often full of plant material, depending on where she is going, plus one vase and her suitcase, she sets out on lengthy journeys, unaware of whom or what awaits her at the journey's end.

This fact alone has singled her out as an exceptional woman, and this book, relating her experiences and depicting her reactions, makes fascinating reading. You know immediately that she has a sense of mission. She has a message to give to ordinary people which is that within ourselves we have skills and untouched talent. All around us is the bounty of nature from which each one of us can create 'pictures' of beauty.

Without any realization of the fact, she belongs to the evangelists of the world. Like them, she gives no thought to personal acclaim or gain. It could be that the difficulties, problems and personal griefs that have beset her life – always met with fortitude and courage – have done a great deal in forming her character, making her oblivious to personal gain and material success.

Those of us who have known her in the world of flower arranging and all its manifestations, bear for her love and respect, not only for her artistic skills but also for her generous and warm personality. She always finds time to commend and encourage others in their work, and to help both our organization (the National Association of Flower Arrangement Societies) and those people who are setting out on their various paths. She shares their successes and will help them through their difficulties.

9

If this conjures up a 'do-gooder', prim and dour, nothing could be further from the truth for she is fun to be with. Julia is blessed with classic good looks, has great elegance, and is full of natural charm. Add to these qualities a great vitality and zest for living which never seems to flag.

There are few more exhausting experiences, more physically demanding, than being involved with the Chelsea Flower Show and having to face the milling throngs of people, the turgid atmosphere generated in a marquee and the frustrations engendered by trying to achieve high standards in a temporary setting. Yet, many times when I have been there with others who, like myself, were feeling spent and exhausted, I have caught sight of Julia threading her way and guiding others through the thick of the crowds, cool and elegant, fresh and full of grace.

As I have read her words in this book, giving her thoughts and reactions to situations and people in different countries, it has seemed to me that she has all the best qualities of the English character: her refusal to be overcome by setbacks and difficulties, her talent for improvisation, and willingness to accept a challenge.

Many people have asked what makes her tick, and the answer invariably is *service* – service to others. Incurably optimistic (obstacles are there to be overcome, she says), she has always been self-confident (she would now call it a confidence of the inner self). This must have helped for it was her passionate talks in the early days that helped get the movement off the ground.

I have enjoyed the whole book and found it absorbing. The visit to Japan raised a few smiles, for I share her respect for their spiritual approach to flower arranging, but how difficult to stifle the British practical approach and the gardener's distaste of an insect bitten leaf. It is almost impossible to see it as a 'symbol of decay in life'.

After the years of dedicated work and pioneering, she richly deserved the Royal Horticultural Society's Victoria Medal of Honour, and the Life Vice-Presidency of the National Association of Flower Arrangement Societies (NAFAS). This was followed by her being presented with the insignia of the Order of the British Empire by Her Majesty the Queen in 1989.

It seems to me that the three roses named in her honour – 'Julia Clements', 'Just Julia', and 'Lady Seton' – epitomize her character. The first, the warm and talented person that she is. The second, her simple non-assertive generous personality, and thirdly, her title 'Lady Seton' which she, typically, has never used to further her career or open doors. Few have known she bore the name of her much loved husband, and were aware only of 'Julia Clements' a distinguished pioneer in the flower world, and author of over twenty books.

This book is not only good reading but also a moving and proud record of an exceptional woman. She has enriched the life of countless people among whom I most certainly include myself.

Iris Webb
Dartmouth 1993
Former president of the
National Association of
Flower Arrangement Societies
(NAFAS)

Preface

'Surely flower arranging must be the fastest-growing interest since the Second World War – I see and hear about it everywhere. How do you account for it?' asked an interviewer at the Taunton flower show fifteen years ago where, with others, I had just finished judging 350 floral-art exhibits.

'I can easily account for it,' I replied, 'for I have played a large part in it but it is a long story.'

'Well, how did *you* start, *when* did you start, *why* did you start, or better still, what *made* you start?' she went on. 'It wasn't here before 1939, was it?'

She made me think and, on reaching home, I sat down at my typewriter, placed a blank sheet of paper in the machine and began to type *My Life With Flowers*. I thought I would relate my travels, which would include the people I have met. After some hours, I realized it would take me a very long time to collect all the details and to write it in between the demands of my daily working life, but I persevered.

Who would have thought that, sitting in a bedsitter after the Second World War (my home had been bombed), at a time when I felt all was lost, that flowers could have taken me round the world and led to such a fulfilling life? What happened to me can happen to anyone: when inspiration comes we must be ready to put our ideas into action.

This is a human story, simply written, about how I began and focusing on flowers and my travels. It is about people and thoughts and gardens and experiences. I hope you will enjoy reading *My Life With Flowers* as much as I have enjoyed writing it.

Julia Clements
Chelsea 1993

PART ONE

PREPARING THE GROUND

1
Early Days
in the United States

I T ALL BEGAN in 1947 when my life really found its purpose.
What I did before then never seemed to have had a real aim,
although I knew I wanted to help people. But let me explain.
During the Second World War I worked for the Red Cross Agricultural Fund and immediately after the war I joined the staff of that
charming magazine called *My Garden*. It was through these two chan-
nels that I received and distributed some of the vegetable seeds that
were sent by American garden clubs to help us grow food.

In 1947, at the time of the International Flower Show in New York, I
was invited to speak at a luncheon there at which 280 garden-club
presidents would be present. The main aim of my attendance was to
say 'Thank you' for all they had done for us during the war.

My excitement was great at the thought of going to the USA,
especially as at that time very few people were allowed to travel or to
take any money out of the country. I had to obtain government permission to finance a two-week stay. This was allowed, as it was felt I
might help by mentioning the Marshall Aid Plan in my talks. (This plan
was introduced in 1947 by George Marshall, then US Secretary of
State, to supply aid for the European recovery programme.)

I managed to gather a few items to wear — we were still strictly
rationed for clothes – but, as the day for my departure drew near, I was
still without a blouse and no one had any coupons to spare. Then I
noticed some torn, fine net curtaining fluttering in the breeze at the top
of my bomb-blasted windows. I took this down, made a blouse out of
it, dipped it in boiling water to which I had added a few drops of
purple ink which dyed it a pale mauve, matching the stripe in my
tweed suit. I was satisfied, and off I set.

I recall my first sight of New York, which was quite frightening. It
now seems strange that I should have felt like that in a city I have since

come to enjoy. But the streets seemed narrower than I had expected and, as I walked down them, I could hardly glimpse the sky between the tall buildings, or so it seemed. There were lights everywhere. I was enthralled, as I had come from power-cut, candle-lit London. (Although some lighting was allowed in 1949, full lighting was not restored until 1952.) Everyone seemed in a rush and, as I sauntered, staring in amazement at almost everything, I was often pushed by hurrying passers-by. I had no strength or confidence to retaliate, I felt so vulnerable in the face of all these confident, well-fed people.

In 1947 I was still bruised by personal losses of my own and shocked by all that had happened during the war. The appalling destruction was deeply imprinted on my mind and I felt low and inadequate. Arriving in New York, I felt more like running home to curl up in my armchair, even if the room was windowless. But I had to go on and, looking back on those first post-war days in New York, I have since been able to understand what it must be like to be a refugee. But I was not a refugee. I had been invited, and warmth and friendship surrounded me. I was bewildered and it took me time to get accustomed to it all.

When I reached the Grand Central Palace, where the luncheon for the International Flower Show was to be held, I stood on the side, aghast, watching the ladies arrive. All were beautifully dressed, with orchid corsages pinned to their shoulders, and many wore mink coats. You can imagine how horrified I felt. Coming from war-torn Britain, I was frightened at this affluence and began to lose my nerve. I started to shake and felt I had not the courage to get up on the platform. With tears in my eyes I went up to the national president, Mrs Helen Waters, and asked if there was some way I could be excused from speaking.

'I had no idea you had such an imposing audience,' I said. 'Just look at all their beautiful clothes and their mink coats. Do you know I am only wearing a curtain?' She put her arm around me and said: 'My dear girl, you are from Britain which stood alone in the war and now you are wanting to back out. You get up there and tell us all about it and, as for our mink coats, why, we'd all give those for your British blood.' So I was pushed on to the platform.

I really can't remember exactly what I said at that flower show in 1947, but it seemed to make a deep impression for at the end I was surrounded by these ladies who asked if I would go to their clubs or conferences to speak or to attend a convention. Having no idea at that time of the size of the USA, I agreed to everything, and gave them my hotel address. When the telephone calls and letters came in I found I had said yes to an invitation in Chicago, followed by one in Virginia and back again to Boston, then another in Chattanooga. On looking at the map I realized that I simply couldn't manage it so, when the lady in New York telephoned me and asked how I was getting on, I told her that I thought I would have to cancel the engagements because I hadn't the money to get to these places. She then asked me what my fee was and, when I explained that I had no fee – I had come only to say thank you, to join hands across the ocean in friendship – she said: 'I had better organize you. I will tell all these people that you will speak for nothing, but they will have to get you from wherever you are to your next appointment.' So it was that I started off in New York and went on to fulfil my other engagements and, in this way, my two weeks' stay extended to several months. Eventually I spoke in twenty-two states, without a penny in my pocket.

My next talk, after the initial one at the flower-show lunch, was to be at the English Speaking Union. I was extremely nervous and as I felt that I looked dowdy, I walked into Saks in Fifth Avenue to buy a new blouse. There I stood behind two ladies who were undecided whether to have short or long sleeves, and whether to have the wrists lace-edged or stitched, or even with turn-back cuffs. I was impatient, for all I needed was a covering and, had I been offered a blouse of sack cloth, I would have taken it. In the event, I bought the first blouse they showed me.

On my travels through the States I noticed the work of the garden clubs and the women's organizations and became very interested in what they were doing in flower arranging. Mrs Lewis Hull, who was the president of the National Council of State garden clubs with its 364,150 members, had taken me under her wing in New York and helped me tremendously to understand their work and aims. Then and now, in addition to the civic plantings they carry out, they maintain hospital gardens, study conservation and bird-protection programmes, organize flower-show schools and wild-flower plantings. I became deeply interested in the Blue Star Highway project, a roadway which runs through several states from west to east and which the garden-club members in each state agree to plant and maintain with indigenous material.

Later, I spent a week in the offices of the Garden Clubs of America, where Mrs Herman G Place, the president at that time, not only gave me private hospitality in her home but also explained the importance of the clubs' aims which were: 'to stimulate the knowledge and love of gardening among amateurs; to share the advantages of association through conference and correspondence in the USA and abroad; to aid in the protection of native plants and birds; and to encourage civic plantings.'

Everyone I met in the USA was so kind, all offering help. One friend delivered a new typewriter to my hotel in New York, saying he had not been able to read all my letters (he did not know that for a long time we were unable to obtain typewriter ribbons). Another friend bought me a slim leather briefcase, gold-initialled, adding that I should not go about with all my papers clutched in my hand – a briefcase, or even a large envelope, had been unobtainable for years at home. Another lady gave me a hundred dollars to go to buy a friend some underwear. She had heard from me earlier that this friend, unable to find material for her wedding dress, had bought a torn silk parachute (no coupons needed), and had unpicked the stitching to enable her to make the dress. The parachute had been recovered from an airman who had been shot down in a field near her home. Yet another lady, at whose home I spoke, said she was changing the uniform of her butlers and chauffeurs and asked if the clothing was of any use to me. I was delighted and had the clothing sent to the mayor of Beckenham, my home town in Kent, where 17,000 houses had been damaged by the V1 bombs and the V2 rockets*. Garden-club ladies everywhere, at whose meetings I spoke, would offer me clothes for myself. Many felt I was 'undressed' because I did not wear gloves (it was the fashion at that time to wear Minnie Mouse short-wrist gloves), and they would go out and buy several pairs for me in various colours.

I lost my bewilderment slowly and everything began to be exciting.
Back at the hotel in between journeys, as I had very little money for
food, I would sit in the lounge watching the guests having tea, sand-
wiches and cakes, with my mouth drooling. When the tea was over the
waitress would wrap up some of the leftovers which I took up to my
room. Our stomachs had shrunk during the years of rationing and I
could not accept all that was offered to me when eating out. Why, I
would ask, serve me two lamb cutlets or two eggs when I had only
asked for one? Then to find that the waiter would throw away the
second one into the garbage bag. I thought of my dog at home who had
never seen meat. One day a friend, hearing about my dog, brought me
some tins of dog meat that I promptly sent home, only to find later that
my family had eaten the meat, thinking it was for them as we did not
have tinned dog food at that time. Yes, I was in another world.

One talk took me to a great estate on Long Island where liveried
servants guided the cars of my audience and where, after my talk, I was
asked to stay as a guest and to join my hostess on her yacht for a cruise.
But, to keep a promise I had made at the flower show in New York, I
went on to my next engagement where I had to share a room with my
hostess, her husband being a night watchman at a nearby factory. I
certainly was meeting a cross-section of the public and it was all so very
interesting.

Over the years I have come to love New York and the Americans. I
know even now that I could never repay all the wonderful hospitality
that has been shown to me and I do not think they expect it. They
wanted to help and were so open and trusting. Editors' doors were
opened to me, circulation figures given, hopes and plans were explained
and I was immediately made to feel one of the family, whether it was in
business or at home. We in Britain seem to take so much longer before
we accept strangers. It is said that in America you are a friend until you
are found out but in Britain you are found out before you are a friend,
and, possibly, this explains the difference between us.

On my return to England I was often asked what I had talked about in
the United States. Well, it was obvious before I left that I might be
invited to talk to garden groups so, looking around for a peg on which

to hang my talks, I decided to develop a thesis I had once written on the history of English gardens. So, before leaving, I had spent three months studying at the British Museum and, with the co-operation of *Country Life* (that wonderful magazine which is almost England), we had prepared a set of enlarged black-and-white mounted photographs which illustrated the main points in the development of our gardens over the ages. These ranged from the days of the monastery gardens, through the Tudor period to the Elizabethan manor houses, then the landscape-gardens period and the Victorian gardens, right up to the Second World War. At this time most gardens were turned over to growing vegetables – and a great change took place around our formerly enclosed gardens with the removal of all the iron railings which were to be melted down to make guns.

During the war, when I was working for the Red Cross in a bombed building in Piccadilly, I used often to wonder whether the American soldiers, who were billeted in the elegant houses opposite Green Park, knew that before the war there had been high iron railings around the park where they played football which would have denied their entry.

Talking to garden clubs, I felt all of this would interest them, but I soon discovered that my story was too remote or, shall I say, too historically factual for, as I was one of the earliest speakers out of England at that time, the audience wanted to know more about the war and the bombing. Often at Question Time I would be asked if I had ever heard a bomb explode. When I explained that I spent the nights for six months in a shelter underneath our house during the heavy raids in London, and that during the day we dodged the bombs as they fell by rushing into doorways or shelters, the whole audience would come alive, asking dozens of questions.

I had to explain that where I lived, in Beckenham, we were ringed by barrage balloons, and every household had to place a bucket of sand and a broom outside, in order to smother the fire bombs as they fell, brushing them into the gutter. I tried, without real knowledge, to describe the difference between the V1 flying bombs, which we could see and hear and the V2 rockets, which were fired from the French coast and were silent. I explained that if you heard the explosion you were safe; if you didn't, you would know nothing about it. It was a V2 that caused the damage to our house: as my sister and I sat huddled in the shelter, I told the audience, we heard this almighty explosion. It was a new noise to us, for we had heard no plane approach. It was eerie, for there was no shouting. We sat in silence clinging to each other in case another explosion occurred, then after some time a voice called out asking if we were all right. I told my audiences that I called back, 'Yes, but how did you get in?' and that the reply was, 'Well, you have no doors or windows and half the house has gone.' The All-Clear sirens sounded and we emerged to discover that the bomb had dropped about 200 yards from us, destroying many houses, with accompanying casualties.

It was these Question Times that gave me my first lesson as a speaker in tuning in to the needs of the audience on the spot, instead of sticking to something that had been prepared in advance. Few appreciated the difficulty that had been experienced in preparing or producing the enlarged photographs I displayed; even less did they know of the trouble taken in producing the informative catalogue. The year of 1947 had been one of the coldest on record in England. There was no fuel and no electric light and the catalogue was beautifully printed in old English type on a hand press by candlelight. We tried to explain that it was unique, almost a museum piece, but I am sure our American audience was too far removed from our problems to understand these difficulties.

There was no air travel to the USA at that time (the regular BOAC service did not commence until October 1958) and although I could enjoy the sea journey after my huge wooden cases, carrying these important mounted photographs, were placed in the hold of the ship marked 'Not Wanted on Journey', I found the crates burdensome especially when I had to move them about physically when travelling by land all over the USA. Many of the groups I visited thought I would be showing coloured slides but, of course, we had no colour films at that time and, in any case, most of the historic gardens I was describing had never been photographed in colour.

I travelled thousands of miles with these large, heavy boxes and had to set up the fifty pictures in whatever venue I found myself. Sometimes I spoke in private homes, at other times in halls, sometimes in night clubs during the day, at other times in churches, and once in a store where I was situated on the fourth floor, back near the lavatories, but always, no matter in what town I found myself, it was the distances from state to state that really amazed me.

I remember one of my early journeys when, on my way to Tennessee, I boarded the train in New York at midnight and when I woke up in the morning to look out of my carriage window, I was excited to see beautiful countryside with bounteously flowering trees that I had never seen before. They were creamy white; others were reddish in colour. I later learned that these were the dogwood trees (*Cornus nuttallii*) and the reddish ones were Judas trees. These trees and the other vegetation held my attention so much that I was reluctant to leave my seat in order to have my breakfast in the dining car. As I sat down a coloured waiter sauntered up to me and, before I looked at the menu, I said: 'This is wonderful country – where are we?' He said, with a slow drawl: 'Virginia ma'am.' So I continued to look out of the window during my meal for I did not want to miss any of the plants that I might see. Afterwards I ran back to my carriage and sat glued to the window.

The countryside seemed to get more incredible as we continued our journey and I hurried again to the dining car for my lunch. The same waiter approached me and again I said: 'This is really lovely countryside – it seems to get better as we go south. Where are we now?' Again, in his slow drawl and without looking up he said: 'Virginia ma'am.' Mistakenly thinking he didn't really know, I said: 'But you said it was Virginia this morning.' 'Yes ma'am,' he replied, 'and it will be Virginia until ten after six tonight.' When I told this to a friend she said: 'And Virginia is the fourteenth *smallest* state in the USA.' The size of the country and some of the differing state laws were facts to which I was quickly becoming accustomed.

I recall one train journey when, on stopping at what I presumed was a station, I called the steward and asked for a drink. 'I am sorry,' he said, 'you're in a dry state.' I sat back and started to read. After about ten minutes it seemed that the train started to move and then stopped again. The waiter approached me and said: 'What would you like to drink?' 'But,' I said, 'you told me I couldn't because we were in a dry state.' 'That's right,' he said, 'but we have just moved across the border into a wet state.' He then added, 'If you are travelling much in this country you should get yourself a flask.'

I was to visit the United States frequently in future. On most of my train journeys there, passengers wanted to open up a conversation with me. Someone would say, 'Are you going far?' and after my reply would say, 'Oh, you're English, are you?' and then rapid questions, such as 'Are you on business or holiday?' would follow. I would reply, hoping that that would close the conversation. But no. . . . 'What line are you in – perhaps I can help?' and so it would continue. Everyone wanted to help. Once, when looking at a newsagent's stall on a street corner in New York, I asked the owner if I could just look at certain magazines, as I could not afford to buy them. 'Yes, take a peek,' he answered, 'are you in this line?' 'I do a bit of writing,' I said. 'Well,' he said, 'don't waste your time on me, you want to go to Madison Avenue and talk to the big boys,' and he gave me several names and addresses. Stories such as these and many others endeared me to the Americans who took me wholeheartedly into their open arms, and I loved it. On that first visit, in 1947, I vowed that, if it were possible, I would return each year. This I have done, with a few exceptions ever since, my flower-talk journeys taking me not only to garden clubs but also to most of the great gardens, parks and cities in the USA. Many of these famous gardens, on estates of wealthy owners, possess well-equipped lecture halls, as I know from experience. Many have become educational centres for horticulture and any visiting specialists, who have something of value to say, are always welcomed as speakers.

Longwood, in Pennsylvania, the former home of Pierre du Pont, was, for me, a joy when I visited nearly twenty years later. Of the 1,000 acres, 350 were, and still are, devoted to ornamental horticulture, spectacular illuminated fountains, and unique conservatories with 25-feet-high Georgian-style windows, sheltering some 20 different styles of garden, growing tens of thousands of flowers and plants.

Huge baskets of seasonal flowers hung from 40-feet-high ceilings, while climbing plants decorated the Palladian columns. Thousands of paper-thin, white green-veined caladium leaves acted as a foreground to cascading white and yellow Japanese chrysanthemums. The sight of thousands of red poinsettias at Christmas time was unforgettable.

I was the fourth in a series of six speakers on that visit in March 1968 when the specially invited guests, in formal dress, wandered down the paths among the thousands of tulips and daffodils. It was an elegant sight. The fountains outside covered a wide area, one fountain throwing a jet of water some 130 feet into the air, thousands of people coming during the summer season to witness the coloured fountain display after dark. In addition to the outside gardens, there was an open-air theatre backed with cascades of climbing roses. The fountain curtain, which was thrown upwards, in changing colours, from the front of the stage at the end of performances, would be the envy of Cecil B de Mille.

I must digress here a little to describe something that could only happen in the USA. Mr Henry du Pont of Winterthur hosted a dinner party before my talk at Longwood. On entering the room, I noticed a lady in a striking apple-green, coral and pink dress, bordered in black down the sides. I remarked upon it and she said: 'Oh, it's only one of those throw-on things you get in Florida.' After my talk, which apparently went well, Mr du Pont offered me a lift back to my hotel, then extended the courtesy to the lady in the brightly coloured dress. As we approached her home, by some means unknown to me at that time, the wrought-iron gates leading to her house were opened automatically and I could also see the front door opening. She said a warm goodbye to me and involuntarily, I said: 'Oh, there goes that lovely dress.' Then like a flash, she tore it off her shoulders and threw it back into the car at me saying: 'Here you are, if you really like it.' She then waved, and walked slowly up the drive in her Bermuda short pants and bra, the butler bowing as he opened the door a little wider for her to enter. I did not know her name, but if she ever reads this, I hope she will accept my belated thanks and those of the many friends who have since borrowed the dress on the occasions it demanded.

Other noteworthy gardens that I visited included the Callaway Gardens in South Carolina, which offers similar facilities to speakers though not on quite such a grand scale, and the theatre in Williamsburg, where the annual garden symposium is held. Williamsburg is the famous colonial city which was settled in 1652 by the English and which became the capital of Virginia. In 1827 parts of this historic place were restored and it is here you can see the houses, shops, gardens, church and Government House, reproduced exactly as they were in colonial days. The Duke Gardens in New Jersey were also unusual: Mrs Doris Duke offers to the public her idea of the many gardens she has admired in the world. You are therefore able to see her view of a Spanish garden with iron grilles and geraniums; an Italian garden set out with water fountains; a Japanese garden with bamboo bridges; a Mexican and an Indian, plus a beautiful representation of an English garden.

The main purpose of my first visit to the USA in 1947 had been to thank the garden clubs for their help to Great Britain during the war. The Victory Garden Scheme had been started there after Pearl Harbor in 1941 to promote some 200,000 gardens, sponsored by the clubs, who were encouraged to supply us and our allies with vegetables.

The scheme had had difficulty in getting underway and, on listening to an appeal while I was there made by one of the American proposers, I felt their aim did not have sufficient interest. In Britain, we were forced to grow vegetables in order to survive but on the other side of the Atlantic this situation was all too remote and the Americans were unable to identify themselves with our need.

When I voiced my opinion of the plan, I was asked to contribute some ideas on the radio and, later still, was linked up to three governors of various states who were running the scheme and who thrust questions at me. I enjoyed the experience of speaking off the cuff, something one could not then do on the radio at the BBC where a script had first to be scrutinized and approved.

I was offered jobs on the radio also, as I travelled round the States. Requests to join a seed firm, a horticultural conglomerate, a garden magazine and women's magazines also came my way.

Finally, however, I announced that I would return home. Mr Lester Norris, the president of the Victory Garden Scheme, together with the secretary, invited me to a farewell dinner in order to express their thanks for the help I had given. I was taken to the 21 Club and, as usual, we were asked to wait in the bar lounge whilst the table was being prepared. The regular palmist approached us and asked if I would like my hand read. I hesitated, but my friends urged me on and passed to her a high-denomination dollar note, so I moved over to her chair and sat beside her. She took my open hand, then heaved a sigh saying I had years of hard work before me. I also sighed, for I had hoped she might tell me of a tall, dark and handsome man, but she continued, giving exact information about my past and my family. She then sighed again and, after a pause, she said: 'You are going to lead a cause, or wave a banner. It is to do with women, I can see them all, and you will have many followers.' I did not pay any attention to this, for nothing in my mind seemed to connect with it. It was only in later years, when travelling around Britain talking to women in clubs, institutes, schools and churches, preaching almost with a passion that flower arranging was a subject that all could do to relieve the post-war doldrums, that I recalled the message of the palmist at the 21 Club.

I wrote back to the club in New York later when I realized the significance of her message but I was never able to trace her.

*Reprisal weapons: V1, a pilotless flying bomb and V2, a long-range rocket that travelled faster than sound.

2

The Beginning – in England

O N MY RETURN home from the States in 1947, I was very much at a crossroads in my life.

In 1945 my home had been bombed, my husband pronounced missing and my baby had been born dead during an air raid when there had been no doctors available and no blood transfusions to spare. It seemed then that all I had ever hoped for was lost.

I was still searching for a meaning to my life. I think, like thousands of other British women, I was longing to help to put the world aright but I didn't know how. I knew that a job for money or a commercial venture for personal reward was not the answer. I desperately wanted to help my own womenfolk. So I came home to a bedsitter in Queensgate, London, where I knew I would have to sit down and plan where I was going.

I had not been home for more than ten days when I had a call from the president of the Kent Area Women's Institute who asked if I would be one of three speakers at their annual All Day Meeting of 400 women in Maidstone, Kent. Would I, she asked, speak on my American experiences? I agreed and planned an hour's talk on my travels, the food I'd eaten, the clothes I'd been given, the work of the garden clubs and other experiences. When I arrived, however, I was appalled at the sight of my own countrywomen. The picture was just the opposite to that which I had seen in the USA, for here the women were shuffling into that great Corn Exchange hall looking down at heel, dispirited and grey, shabbily dressed and almost, it seemed, without hope. I looked around wondering what I could do about it. I felt I had to do or say something, but at that moment the president was hurrying me to take my place on the platform with the other two speakers.

She introduced the first speaker whose subject was 'Make-do and Mend', a subject we had had drummed into us during the war years. The second speaker had been sent by the Ministry of Agriculture to explain how to fill in the new chicken-ration form whereby we could obtain meal for as many chickens as we wanted to breed, provided we gave the eggs to the government official, bar the one a week we could keep for ourselves. I was shocked.

The talk I had already prepared did not seem to be appropriate to the situation as I saw it. I was in mental torment, trying to think what I ought to say that could lighten the atmosphere positively, when I heard I was being introduced. My name sounded as though it was coming from afar – I seemed not to be there. I stood up and looked up, almost with an inner cry for help. It came. I put down my prepared notes and said:

'I have listened to these two very excellent speeches but I can't believe, having just come back from the USA, that you who have won the war, and have been in the front line in Kent, having faced the bombardment and the V1s and V2s, are still having to listen to talks about rationing and quotas and under-the-counter goods. Everything seems so negative, there must be something positive that we can do.'

I then remembered the small, simple flower arrangements I had seen in the American garden clubs, made with a tall branch and a few flowers, so unlike the masses of flowers we used for special occasions in England before the war. I looked down at the customary bowl of flowers placed on the president's table and the answer came to me in a flash.

'Flowers,' I cried. 'Flowers we have in great abundance and in greater variety than almost any other country in the world. These are not rationed, or restricted, they are not even held back for export. They are here, free for everyone. We could all be artists with flowers.' Then, without any real knowledge, I picked up a few flowers, put them in my hand in some order, remembering school art lessons about different forms, shapes and sizes, and said: 'You do not always need a mass of flowers. This is all you need do: just place a tall one or two for height, some medium ones lower down, and some short ones low down, then you can add some pieces of wood, or stones in the dish or even an ornament if you like, but make a picture of your choice. Do not just put a bunch of flowers in a jar of water, then get on with some other chore – in that way you are only giving them a drink and are not obtaining any expression for yourself. Open your eyes and look at their different forms and shapes and colours. Every one of us is different, so we can each make a different picture. Some of you may like pink and blue, others red and yellow, some may like tall flowers, others short, but be yourself – be expressive. This will encourage you to open your eyes to the tremendous possibilities of creating with flowers. Even in the depth of winter you can still use a bare branch for height, some leaves in between and some cones or fruit low down, but start now by becoming an artist with flowers, for it is an expressive and rewarding subject and, with the changing seasons, never ending in interest.'

I continued talking like this, gathering strength of purpose, and began to feel like a lion on a soap box. I became so excited that I did not notice the time, but when I had finished I was surrounded by the women, many of whom asked if I could please go and talk to their institutes or conferences.

This may all sound odd today when hundreds of thousands of people practise the art of flower arranging all the year round. But it must be remembered that at that time there was no, or very little, commercial growing of flowers and no imports from other lands. There was little fuel to heat greenhouses and, except for those with access to greenery and dried ferns, flower arranging as a subject for everyone was non-existent.

I was invited all over the country. I nodded and gave people my address, returning to my rooms that night utterly exhausted but exhilarated. I sat down on my bed, looked up and said: 'Thank you, I think I know now where I am going.'

I was now filled with ambition to accept the challenge of helping my fellow countrywomen. I had no premises or equipment and no money, but nothing would stop me. I knew I had to go ahead. I didn't even stop to think whether I knew enough about the subject or whether it would pay me. I was just convinced that I had to go out and speak to others about flowers. I was sure that I would be guided.

At first I went to the bombed cities, including Dover, Southampton, Newcastle, Liverpool and Birmingham, and everywhere I went there was a cry for more. I bought the flowers in the place where I was speaking in order not to deter the audience by using flowers they could not obtain. Vases were scarce after the war so I took oven dishes, casseroles, teapots or any household item that would hold water, for these were not on quota or restricted.

I did not look into the future, I just acted on the spur of the moment but it was exhilarating and I was always overjoyed at the enthusiasm of the audiences. I did not want them to sit and watch, I wanted them to participate, and to achieve by going home to make a picture with their flowers. For simplicity's sake I did not use horticultural terms. Holding a spray of flowers in my hand, I'd say: 'If it is long and thin, place it on the outside of your pattern, if it is round or more dominant put it in the centre, and fill in with the rest.' I made it appear very easy. Many leaving the meeting would say: 'I could have done that,' and so of course they could, but the idea was positive, unlike everything else at that time which was either unobtainable or viewed in the negative.

Flowers had always been used decoratively before the war but mainly in great houses where rare specimens from the greenhouses were often displayed. Large groups of flowers were the main decoration at banquets and society weddings, but they were the work of professionals. Now it was the war-weary women who needed help, women who had previously stood in awe before these lavish displays thinking flower arranging was not for them. 'But flowers are free for everyone. We could all be artists with flowers,' I stressed. 'Whether you have a small or a large garden or, if none at all, there is always the countryside, and flowers are not on coupons. If your eyes are open,' I constantly reminded them, 'assessing flowers in terms of their shapes, and sizes and colours, to make a living picture, could be both exciting and rewarding.'

At first I thought the interest would only last a few months, but the demands for talks and demonstrations became even more numerous and then snowballed. I knew then that I had discovered my vocation. I was also mobile with no home ties. Was this, I sometimes wondered, a consolation for that which I had lost? Was I meant to lose, to enable me to do this? As I went around, sometimes scrambling over rubble in order to reach the often windowless venue, I wondered how better I could get my ideas across to large groups of people. I had to devise some kind of simple basic advice. I finally decided to work with 'threes', that is, tall, medium and short. In other words, by identifying tall, medium and short flowers and leaves, and by thinking of flowers in the framework of points, rounds or flats, anyone, and I emphasized *anyone*, could arrange flowers. More creative work would come later, I explained, but it was the simple start that was necessary.

Everywhere I went the audience left me inspired and full of commitment. I could not keep up with the demand for talks, which I was now receiving at about twenty a week. I needed help so, through the gardening press, I invited ladies to attend an instructional course, provided they would promise to pass on to others any help they gained. In other words, my aim was not to help those who wanted to do flowers for parties, but to find those who would go out and help the war-weary women find themselves. These women, some of whom became famous, could all tell their own stories, for they worked extremely hard in those early days.

The fact that there was something expressive, something positive everyone could do, spread all over the country — it was like an explosion — and the more I spoke and trained others the more the interest increased, finally reaching a point when I decided to write a newsletter to help keep everyone together. I also wrote a leaflet entitled 'How to form a Flower Club', devised innumerable schedules and organized shows. The following year, more organization was required. In 1952, I formed a Judges' School to establish the principles of judging floral art.

As I travelled alone I knew I could only leave a mark for others to build on. The demand for knowledge and instruction was urgent, but how to disperse it was an even greater problem. I thought a book might do it, so then came my first effort, which is a story in itself.

The late Theo Stephens, then a director of *Country Life* and chairman of Newnes Pearson, sums this up in his Foreword to my tenth book *Fun with Cut Flowers*, published in 1961.* I quote:

I have always been an optimist, often to my cost; but when, in 1949, Julia Clements suggested that I should publish her first book on flower arranging, so aptly titled *Fun With Flowers,*** I hesitated. My first reaction was to wonder whether her enthusiasm for the subject was not swamping my sense of publishing realism.

But Julia was unwavering in her belief in the future of flower arranging. She was not to be deterred and she may even have bullied me a little! Finally, I agreed to take the risk and publish a first edition of 5,000 copies. Even then she was not satisfied and so great was her enthusiasm that before going to press I increased the print order, not without some qualms, to 10,000 copies. I was wrong, for in a few months I had to print a further 10,000.

The book eventually sold 90,000 copies before going out of print to make way for my second and third titles.

Fun With Flowers only served to spread the interest even further. Letters started to come in from Europe and countries further afield including, eventually, an invitation to visit New Zealand. My work had begun. It was the beginning of my meeting all those wonderful people, of my travels to far-away places, of coming to know and love those famous gardens and unusual flowers – in other words, of my life with flowers.

*Published by Pearson in 1961.
**Published by *My Garden* and C Arthur Pearson in 1950.

3

New York Interlude

I N THE SPRING of 1948 I was to return to the United States to give talks at the International Flower Show in New York and was given space both to display pictures of English gardens and to represent *My Garden*. Coming as I did from Britain, the president of the show, Mr Richardson Wright, who was also garden editor of *House and Garden*, asked if I would display an orchid that had come from the top of Princess Elizabeth's wedding cake and that had been sent to him by a guest at the royal wedding. It had arrived in a gas-mask case, since no boxes or other packing materials were available.

I replied in wonderment, asking how he could possibly show an orchid in the spring of 1948 which had been cut the previous November, the date of the royal wedding. He then explained that the orchid had been dehydrated by the New York Botanical Gardens by burying it in a box which contained powdered borax. I was shown the dehydrated flower which looked like parchment but was still in its original form, and eventually I agreed since the organizers wanted it used for publicity purposes. I went to an antique shop and was loaned a glass dome. I then bought a small piece of black velvet on which I laid the orchid and covered it with the dome. I asked the signwriters of the show to make me a card explaining the origin of the bloom and its method of preservation. They did this in great style, finishing with a crown at the head of the notice. With the orchid set in the centre of an antique table and the framed recipe on the one side, on the other I placed a photograph of Princess Elizabeth and Prince Philip, which I had obtained from the British Information Services. I did not imagine anyone would really stop to look at it, so went ahead with my own programme. However, I did not reckon with the publicity office, for when the press arrived the next morning they were handed a sheet on which all the special exhibits were mentioned. At the end it was stated that an orchid from Princess Elizabeth's wedding cake had been preserved and was on display on the fourth floor.

My position in the show was on the fourth floor right at the back, where I imagined that no one would ever find me, so you can imagine my surprise when during the press preview the whole of the press corps descended upon me. 'Where's the orchid?' they shouted, as they pushed and held their cameras up high. When I removed it from its glass case, there was almost a fight to get an exclusive shot of it. I was photographed with it in my hair, on my lapel and at all kinds of angles. Some of the photographers brought their fashion models with them and, in turn, they were photographed with the orchid, looking up or down at it, and all the time I was afraid it might break. The story of the orchid's preservation together with photographs appeared in all the papers which, of course, pleased the organizers of the show. Crowds arrived for admission the next day all wanting to know where the orchid was.

So great was the demand at the information desk that a red tape was fixed from the ground floor up the stairways to the back of the fourth floor indicating, 'To the Royal Orchid'. The crowds queued to pass in line before this dehydrated orchid and instead of selling *My Garden* I was reduced to smiling and saying: 'Move along please.' In the crowd a coloured lady came up to me and gazed longingly at the photograph of the royal couple. She begged me to let her have it but, even when I explained that it was my only copy, she still would not move away. Finally I said I would try to get another one, and off she went. The British Information Services printed me a hundred copies of the photograph of the royal couple which I sold for a dollar each (I could easily have sold a thousand). The next day this lady approached me with the words: 'And now can I have a picture?' As she had paid another two dollars to get into the show, I was happy to give her one. She hugged it close to her and then said: 'You see, I wanted it badly, for she is *my* princess as well as yours. I am from Jamaica.'

On my return to England in the summer — still 1948 — I picked a number of flowers and preserved them in powdered borax adding a little alum to the mixture. I also pressed leaves between newspaper, using a warm iron. Remembering the enthusiasm in New York, I asked the Royal Horticultural Society if I could stage a display of dried flowers. My request was refused, it being explained that as a learned society dealing with living plants they could not foresee space being given up to a display of dried decorations. I was too soon.

However, I did hire the lecture room in the RHS building in 1952 and announced in the gardening press that I would give a day's course on dried-flower arrangements. I displayed and labelled about thirty different flowers and made ten dried-flower decorations. One hundred and fifty people attended and I am sure those early pioneers will remember the day. But how times have changed for, since then, some of the best exhibitions of dried-flower decorations have taken place in the great halls of the Royal Horticultural Society.

I included a chapter on the four different methods of drying flowers in one of my early books* and since then many other books have been written. I am often astounded at the imagination used by many of the exhibitors of dried flowers whose work I have seen at shows. The creation of collages, pressed-flower pictures, plaques, samplers, insignias, posies and large mass arrangements, which by their colouring and composition are truly works of art, have provided a creative outlet to many who previously have never looked into the heart of a flower. Little did I realize as I held up that dried-out orchid in New York in 1948 that such a vast development of this art would ensue. Since that time the introduction of the desiccant silica gel has made the drying of flowers more popular, in fact by the quick drying of flowers in the microwave ovens, it has become a big business.

There was also a sequel to the American interest in English gardens and royal flowers. In the year following the display of the royal orchid, the magazine *Country Life* took an 'island site' at the show in New York which was tastefully decorated with gilt-framed pictures of stately homes, gardens, and royal purple settings, displaying models of the crown, orb and sceptre. The magazine *My Garden*, at one end of the site, displayed garden material and pictures, and I was on hand to answer questions and give talks.

So great was the enthusiasm for British gardens, and so many requests were received for me to organize tours (one group asking if I could arrange for them to charter a yacht which would take them round the coast of Britain to visit various gardens), that it all became too much. On my return to London, I passed over this side of things to the British Travel Authority, and together with the editor of *My Garden*, we wrote the first BTA leaflet entitled 'Come to Britain's Gardens'. This led to the opening of the BTA's New York office with Mr James Turbayne, who was always such a help to me when I was in that great country, as its head.

101 Ideas for Flower Arrangements published by C Arthur Pearson in 1953.

PART TWO

THE SEEDS ARE SOWN

4

Canada

IN 1949 I WAS again in North America. This time I was in Vancouver where I boarded the Canadian Pacific train that would take me the almost 3,000-mile journey through the Rockies to Toronto where I was due to judge, speak and demonstrate.

We all have mental pictures of famous sights we hope one day to see but it is not often that the real thing comes up to expectations. The range of snow-capped mountains that extend for 600 miles, known as the Canadian Rockies, surpassed my wildest imaginings.

Looking back, as I sit comfortably at home, I feel the human mind can hardly grasp their greatness except by some comparison, so it is well to ponder on the fact that it takes the fastest Canadian Pacific train three days and nights to go from Mission, where the real Rockies begin, to Cochrane where they finish, yet it takes the Orient Express only five hours to traverse the length of the Swiss Alps. The Rockies have been described as fifty Switzerlands rolled into one, and certainly this is no exaggeration.

My eyes were glued to the window, mentally making many notes. I was particularly struck at one point by a little wooden arch, spanning a stream, on which was written in large white letters 'The Great Divide'. It looked so insignificant against the massive background of the huge mountains but it marked the boundary between the state of British Columbia and that of Alberta, the stream running east towards the Atlantic and west to the Pacific Ocean.

Another magnificent sight was Lake Louise looking like a shimmering jewel – guarded by the rugged mountains that stood like sentinels all round it with the famous turreted Château Hotel, which housed 700 guests, nearby on the shore. I left the train here in order to stay one night amid the luxury of this beautiful hotel, the gardens of which were full of flowers in summer, mainly poppies surrounding the lake. The next day I picked up the train to continue my journey.

A short distance further on, Mount Eisenhower rose like a mighty fortress. Travelling companions told me this one mountain is 800 miles long and 9,400 feet high (and is not the highest in the range). Originally known as Castle Mountain, it was renamed in 1946 as a Canadian tribute to the great American general. When you realize that Snowdon, the highest mountain in Wales, is 3,560 feet, it will give you some idea of the size of this bastion-like monarch of the Rockies.

At times I was almost tired of the constant snow and mountains, rather as I imagine the Arabs get tired of the heat and sand, but on this journey a passenger had the relief of an attractively upholstered cabin with settee and table, on which illustrated menus, describing the scenery through which we might pass, were placed before every meal. Then there was the observation car and bar – a happy meeting place at any time where many discussions took place and friendships made.

Most of the passengers were businessmen, but one man, asking if I were on business or pleasure, extended his hand when I said 'flowers', adding that his wife was a president of a garden club back in Buffalo (in New York State). Our talk continued for a while along these lines but it seemed strange that flowers should be our topic among all those men. As we journeyed I was struck by the lovely town of Banff which sits in a valley with the impressive Cascade Mountains as a background. It was difficult to appreciate that, although the roads and houses were thickly covered in snow, here were to be found some of the finest hot springs on the continent. You can swim in warm sulphur water all the year round, for a million gallons flow from springs each day at a temperature of 90°F (32°C).

The train runs on through this magnificent scenery hour after hour – there seemed no end to it – snowy peaks, vast icefields, glaciers, foaming torrents of water, canyons and blue-water lakes that look like vast sapphires against the glittering white of the snow. All this is there to be absorbed on one train journey. I found it was impossible to do so – there was just too much to see.

As we approached the flat lands of the prairies, I looked back on the last notable sight of the Rockies, the peaks of the Three Sisters, each nearly 10,000 feet high. The invincible might of these mountains told me something about the courageous and dogged spirits of the pioneers who built the railway through this formidable country over seventy years ago.

I arrived in Toronto with a day to spare before joining the panel of judges at the Garden Club of Toronto Flower Show. It was snowing and I was met in the entrance hall of the O'Keefe Centre by several ladies swathed in fur, which meant luxury to me. I was surprised later to find they had discarded their coats and all appeared in bright yellow working smocks to set up the competitive classes in horticulture and flower arranging, as well as the boutique for handcrafted floral gifts, dried flowers, herbal and wine jellies. A good show of democracy I thought.

I found the staging of the flower-arrangement classes different and exciting, and enjoyed the judging tremendously, a pleasure which was only exceeded later when I saw the well-appointed auditorium at the Civic Garden Centre where I was to give a demonstration. It looked like a small theatre with a raised stage so that all could see, and so different from the many war-damaged church halls in England just after the war. This centre, initiated and supported by the garden club, was set in a carefully tended park owned by Metropolitan Toronto. It was, and still is, an independent, self-supporting organization, used by the garden club for its lectures on horticulture, landscaping, conservation and flower arranging. There was also a shop containing all the necessary items for flower arranging and garden, in fact it was a centre in the real sense of the word. I was shown round by Mrs Douglas Bryce, who took me first to the Scented Garden for the Blind which the club created and maintained. I was interested in the winding paths flanked each side by $2\frac{1}{2}$-feet-high walls which hold the garden at touching level. All the plants were scented, of different textures and all labelled in Braille.

Another of the club's projects was the Enchanted Garden for disabled children. Here I saw young children climbing ladders and sliding down chutes, some armless, wearing crash helmets. There was a tree house and all kinds of mounds and grassy banks topped by trees, planted there for climbing. I paused to think how much more worthy it was for the garden-club members to be involved in their community, than just to sit and watch others at demonstrations.

Certain highlights stand out in everyone's travels and on a later visit to Canada, in 1967, two come to mind as I write. The first was a memorable visit to Niagara Falls, over whose thunderous waters a rainbow constantly hovered. The other was not as awesome but nevertheless just as unusual. I was sitting at a semi-official dinner given in my honour at the end of a show in Toronto by Mrs Lois Wilson, the president, and her husband, when I happened to remark that I regretted being unable to visit the forthcoming Expo 67 in Montreal as I was leaving the next day. This seemed to be no trouble to one John Bradshaw, gardening broadcaster and a guest at table, who said if I really wanted to go, he could arrange for me to be picked up, then added: 'If you agree, you will have to leave fairly soon to take the 10 pm plane to Montreal.' I hesitated, not wishing to break up the party, but my hosts said it was a great chance and should not be missed. Then followed a few telephone calls and I left the dinner party, was rushed to the airport, where I was told I was to stay the night at the Montreal Airport hotel. At 7 am the next morning I was to go to the breakfast room to meet the crew of XYH 20 who would fly me by helicopter over the site of Expo 67 in Montreal.

I followed my instructions, asking at several tables in the morning if the occupants were XYH 20. I finally made contact and we took off, flying over the rooftops of the city. I learned that the crew were traffic reporters of the city's radio station, reporting on traffic congestions, accidents and snowfalls. After skimming rooftops and dodging church spires, we came down on the site of the unfinished show, where I was received with flowers and taken round the pavilions by officials. The show at that time was attracting worldwide attention as all nations of the world were taking part, so I was very happy to have had this experience. I was picked up later and taken to the airport where I flew back to Toronto, collected my luggage, and later flew on to New York in readiness for a visit, two days later, to the Chicago Show.

Much has happened since my first visit to Canada. The Garden Club of Toronto's many projects vary from restoring a nineteenth-century garden to continuing to support the Civic Garden Centre which serves the public not only with information on gardening, but also by giving courses and demonstrations. The club also provides a potting shed for the Metropolitan Toronto Zoo to propagate the appropriate plants for the different climatic zoological zones, plus many other worthy activities, all paid for by their shows and other work.

Talking to Katie May McCarthy, the president of the World Show of Flower Arrangement held in Toronto in June 1993, I learned that they have recently renovated the gardens of Casa Loma known as Toronto's Landmark Castle. To do this they raised 1.5 million Canadian dollars (about £750,000 at the time of writing) and worked closely with the landscape architects. They supervised the construction of the flower beds, the fountains and gardens and did a lot of the planting. It must have been satisfying to see what was an overgrown hillside transformed into a beautiful, formal terraced garden and natural woodland dell overlooking the towers of downtown Toronto. It was their gift to the city and must set an example for other garden clubs to follow.

There are now 375 members in the Toronto Club practising flower arranging and horticulture, but this is only one of the fourteen garden clubs in the province of Ontario, all self-supporting. In addition, there are about 258 horticultural societies in the province all affiliated to the Ontario Horticultural Association, which is government supported. The societies practise horticulture and some flower arranging. There is now a Canada-wide Registry of Garden Clubs but, in a country 4,000 miles wide with a population of only 26 million people, Mrs George Frost, the president of the Garden Clubs of Ontario told me that organization is not easy, for the tendency is to divide into regions which are more heavily populated. However, they continue to grow and to flourish.

5

The United States

I HAD A DEFINITE preconceived idea of what Chicago would be like, nurtured, I suppose, by radio, television and newspapers. We had been fed for years on the stories of gangsters, of street shoot-outs, of Al Capone and his moll so, when I knew I had to spend a day in Chicago while waiting for the night train to Arkansas on my first visit to that city in 1950, I felt I should play safe. I called a taxi and asked the driver to take me to the best hotel where I could pass the day safely. On the long drive to the Blackstone Hotel, the driver told me all about his marital problems and how the psychiatrist was dealing with them, then asked me my opinion. I am afraid I was of little help for I was intent on getting to the hotel as quickly as I could.

I deposited my suitcase in the cloakroom, then sat in the lounge afraid to go out until about noon. Thinking I would like a drink to while away the time, I went into the bar, and walked up to the counter. 'Sorry madam,' the barman said, 'I cannot serve you unescorted.' This was a shock coming from the land of Al Capone and I hardly knew where to turn when two men sitting at the bar appeared ready and willing to offer me a drink on hearing my English voice. I was embarrassed, so I asked the barman how it was possible to obtain a drink. 'Only if you eat,' he replied. So, hoping I could do so unnoticed, I slid to a seat at the back of the bar lounge and eventually ordered a meal and a drink which I consumed behind a newspaper. So much for preconceived ideas.

Since that first encounter, I have grown fond of Chicago. It is an incredible city with its superb Lakeside Drive and tall buildings, at night all aglitter with lights like a fairyland. I have been made welcome by the garden clubs and especially by the Chicago Horticultural Society who stage a magnificent flower and garden show each year. It is termed the 'Largest Under-Cover Show in the World' the space covering seven acres and to which some 200,000 people flock in

March to get a glimpse of spring. But plans for my visit did not always go right and to describe the difficulties I can do no better than to quote verbatim from an article that Mr Robert Wintz, the organizer, wrote in the magazine of the New York Botanical Society. He refers to the time ten years earlier when I was scheduled to arrive at the show staged in McCormich Place. Alas, the building was burned down a few weeks previously and the show had to be transferred at speed to the site of the disbanded stockyards where the inn, famous in the days of the beef farmers, was now almost derelict. But I will let him tell the story. He wrote:

It was one of the years the flower show was at the amphitheatre of the stockyards that the Chicago Horticultural Society achieved a milestone of sorts in lecture presentation.

Over the years the Horticultural Society's flower show has had many out-of-state and foreign visitors. They've come to see, judge and participate in many ways. One visitor came to us from Britain: Lady Seton (Julia Clements), one of England's most prominent horticulturists. Our flower show chairman and his wife had been to England earlier in the year, had met Lady Seton and had extended an invitation to her to come to the flower show and give a lecture to members and friends of the Horticultural Society.

Our efforts set British-American relations back that year. There was the late plane, a mix-up in meeting Lady Seton at O'Hare Airport, and an hour and a half taxi ride from O'Hare.

There was also the room at the Stockyards Inn. The Inn, a monument to Chicago's glorious wild west days, was strong on ambience but not on personal comfort. Lady Seton got one of the better rooms — one with a lock on the door and a bathtub in the room.

As I recall, the wind was out of the southwest that night, and it wafted in, redolent with the heady aroma of the stockyards and sharp with the penetrating cold of mid-March. The windows were broken, some stuffed up with newspaper. The quotes to the press the next day are not quite coherent in their entirety but there are clear references to 'stench', 'frozen to the bone' and 'nothing but a horse blanket to keep me warm'.

In addition, in the morning the breakfast rolls were stale, the coffee cream had long since soured, the show chairman was caught in a monumental traffic jam – all while the mayor, who was to open the show, was expected at the amphitheatre exhibit hall momentarily.

The great pigeon caper

Fresh rolls and potable cream were brought, the mayor was welcomed and the show opened. Heading back for the lecture at the Inn's elegant banquet hall, we anticipated relaxing and enjoying Lady Seton's talk. Instead, from the lecture hall came a great commotion and flurry of activity. Could chaos have been re-established? Our worst fears were confirmed when we saw a waiter emerge, tray in hand, ceremoniously carrying out a dead pigeon.

The story of what had happened soon unfolded. Somehow the bird had managed to come in through a broken pane in the skylight and was flying back and forth up at the ceiling. The lecture was delayed and a waiter had to do something about removing the interloper. The waiter reappeared carrying a rifle. With great aplomb he knocked the bird off with one shot. Another waiter then scooped the fallen bird onto his tray and bore it away. You can imagine what an effect this commotion and the shooting of the bird had on my morale.

Order restored, the lecture continued without further interruption. One of our members invited Lady Seton to spend that night as her house-guest and recuperate before the next stop on her tour.

Now, ten years later, I am happy to report that the Society and the flower show are back in the good graces of Lady Seton, who returned to Chicago during our salute to the Bicentennial as our guest. Fortunately, during her return visit the accommodations were more prudently chosen and all pigeons had been re-routed over the lake.

The person who offered me private hospitality was none other than the president of the show, the world-famous architect, Mr I W Colburn, and I would willingly have suffered ten nights under a horse blanket had I known the prize would have been a visit to his famous home, for never before or since have I enjoyed the stark amazement of such a unique building. He and his charming wife looked after me well but, alas, I had to move on.

I returned to Chicago some years later at the invitation of Barclays Bank International whose director, Mr Robin Parr, was the president of the show. Barclays were staging an English garden in the show in which I was to demonstrate English flower arrangements twice a day. This I could not have done without the care and unselfish help of my dear friend the late Bill Kistler, director of the American School of Floral Art, who took me to stores, markets and wholesalers to buy flowers.* I say 'buy' but I was never allowed to pay for them, the wholesalers saying that as I was promoting their flowers, they should be paying me. There were the usual radio, newspaper and television interviews, and there was little time to absorb all that was happening at the show, although I was struck by the amazing beauty of an avenue of acacia (mimosa) trees, all in bloom and emitting their delicate fragrance. I also met and chatted daily with the members of the garden clubs who had staged the flower-arrangement section of the show and I learned that in the state of Illinois alone there were 263 garden clubs affiliated to the National Council.

Yes, my impression of this city, with its population of nearly three million people, has changed greatly since my first visit over forty years ago. Was this really Al Capone's stomping ground? To me, its sparkling lights and water made it a fairyland.

It was over forty years ago also that I went to Chattanooga. I was sitting quietly one evening in New York when I received a telephone call from a lady there to ask me if I would catch a plane the next morning in order to speak to her garden club in the afternoon. She explained that a ticket would be waiting for me at the airport if I agreed, and that I would be met on arrival.

I took an early plane to Chattanooga where I heard the name Clements being called so, knowing I was to be met by someone who did not know me, I almost ran to a stewardess, saying, 'Here I am.' She rushed me to a car which the chauffeur quickly drove off. We stopped outside a building on the steps of which several smiling men were standing in anticipation, so I just smiled back and walked past them into the entrance hall, looking for someone to greet me, then on into a large room where a hundred or more men were seated at lunch tables. I immediately sensed something was wrong – I discovered that I was in a men's Rotary luncheon meeting and they were expecting a Senator Clements from Alabama as speaker. I explained the position but they told me to wait whilst they sent a car to pick up the senator and to find the lady who was to have greeted *me*. They were both brought back to the luncheon meeting. In the meantime, the organizers, having learned where I was from begged me to stay and to say something, as no speaker had reached them from England since the end of the war. My hostess was asked to return for me at 2 pm (my garden-club meeting was due at 3 pm) and I was placed at the top table where I was served with a huge rib steak which dripped over the sides of the wide oval plate. I couldn't face it, thinking it would have been more than enough for a family for a week at home, and I asked for a one-egg omelette. It was later explained to me that the steaks were a gift from the president to each of one of the members.

After the Senator had spoken admirably on some topic which was obviously important to the members, I was asked to speak, or more correctly, to answer the many questions about post-war England that were thrust at me: 'If you are so poor in England why do you pay the royal family?' 'Why are we still sending food parcels to England now that the war is over?' I was able to reply quite effectively for I received a twice-weekly bulletin from the British Information Services giving me not only up-to-date news but also suggestions or, better still, answers to the many questions that were uppermost in the minds of many Americans, especially those who lived at a distance from New York. I was therefore able to say that our royal family cost less than their president and that our royal family, and all it stood for, was a great tourist attraction and brought in revenue.

Many Americans in the Mid-West at that time did not realize that Britain had continued to fight the war alone when the countries of Europe had fallen and that men, women and children had fought with every resource available until these were absolutely depleted; also that, as an island, we had not been able to feed ourselves and little had come in through submarine-infested seas and that, whereas the countries in

Europe were occupied by the enemy, Britain was still fighting whilst being bombed day and night. Europe had lights on and food after the war years before Britain did. I went on in this vein and at the end I was cheered for so long that they nearly missed their afternoon business and I my garden-club engagement.

Anyway, it all went very well and, although I am not sure if I set a record for a woman to speak at a men's Rotary luncheon, I know the next morning smiles greeted me everywhere I went – it seemed I had made friends with everyone in Chattanooga. My own garden-club talk also went very happily and endeared me to a city which I previously had only thought was the name of a Choo Choo.

Writing of things that could only possibly happen in America, I recall leaving the Philadelphia Flower Show once, anxious to catch a train back to New York where I was to connect with a plane back to London. I stood outside the show waiting for a taxi but, as none appeared and thinking I might miss my train, I went up to a policeman and told him of my dilemma, asking how I could possibly find a taxi. 'No problem,' he said, and immediately blew a whistle. Then from a side street a police car appeared. I was told to jump in, and was then whisked at high speed, with klaxons blaring, to the station. I caught my train and the plane; and guess what our conversation was on the way to the station – Dr Billy Graham and, yes, flowers.

Going south again many years later, in 1972, to Atlanta in Georgia I was to stay with Louise Hastings of the famous Donald Hastings Seed Company. Louise, a dynamo if there ever was one, had organized a full-day garden-and-flower event, and my appearance was to be a special one. The mayor and other dignitaries had been invited, a large concert hall had been rented, and I was to demonstrate flowers and period furniture. The stage setting was to be a surprise to the audience, for I was to arrange some flowers on the furniture that was on the floor of the orchestra pit, which was well below floor level and hidden from the audience. The idea was that the furniture would be set out as for a period room and that, after the introduction, on the press of a button, I would rise with the platform, furniture and flowers, acting as though I had just finished a large pedestal arrangement.

The tension was great. The furniture, which I borrowed from Rich's Store, was late in arriving, and as some of it was not of the period for which I had asked, it would not now fit in authentically with the flowers and vases that I intended to use, but somehow I managed. It was dark down below and I was groping about trying to place vases and equipment in a spot where I could easily find them when I reached the full light of the stage above.

My appearance was the last item in a day-long programme, previous experts having discoursed on conservation, gardening in general, indoor plants and the history of gardens. As my time drew near I went below, holding my nerves in reserve as the minutes ticked by. Then, in a loud, amplified voice I heard myself being introduced. I quickly patted my hair and took up my position by the pedestal, waiting for my ride up to platform level. I heard the buzz, the platform shuddered but nothing happened. I heard another buzz and still nothing happened. Yes, there was a fault in the mechanism and I was left in the dark below. I heard a call for an engineer so, in the meantime, I made my way up to the platform and, in an impromptu manner, gave an interim talk on the fascinating art of arranging flowers. The fault was rectified after ten minutes. I descended to the dark again and, finally and triumphantly, rose but of course the surprise was lost.

Looking at this prosperous city today, it is hard to believe that a little more than 120 years ago Atlanta was burned to the ground. It was in 1864 that, during the American Civil War, it was bombarded for two months before it fell to General Sherman. Through the story of *Gone With the Wind* most of us know about the almost total destruction of the city. Only 400 buildings out of some 4,500 were left standing, and those unsteadily. Yet, today, with its imposing skyscrapers, its theatres and ballet, its throbbing business centre and its beautiful parks and gardens, serving two and a half million people, it is a most stimulating city to visit.

I never fail to enjoy my stays in Atlanta, talking to the many garden clubs that exist there, many of which are sponsored by the Atlanta Federal Savings and Loan, now the Georgia Federal Bank, which not only runs a speakers' service to the many garden clubs in the district, but which also sponsored the forum at which I spoke in 1972. What a good example for some of our banks to follow.

*Bill Kistler subsequently opened a branch of the school in Taiwan to which I was invited.

6

Atlantic Crossings

M Y EARLY VISITS to the garden clubs in the USA were made by sea aboard the *Queen Elizabeth*, the *Queen Mary*, or the *Mauretania* and the excitement of four and a half days at sea, in what seemed to be no man's land, has never been matched for me by any other form of travel. The rush to look down the passenger list to see if any friends were on board, the unpacking and arranging of my cabin and watching the baskets and bowls of flowers being delivered to various cabins always made my heart beat a little faster, in anticipation of what, I did not know. I have always been an optimist, feeling that something interesting could happen if I kept my eyes open. I loved those sea journeys and am only so sorry that many people today do not have the opportunity (or perhaps the time) to experience them.

On my first voyage, in 1947, my dining table was next to that of David Niven, who was travelling with his new bride, Hjordis, and his two young sons. Always witty and amusing he would place a table napkin over his arm, acting as a waiter, and would say to each of the boys in turn: 'Are you ready to order, sir?' And to his wife he would add, 'And what would you like, madam?' This would amuse the young boys every time it was repeated. He would also often present his bride with a posy of flowers, taken from a nearby empty table.

On the same crossing was Rex Harrison to whom I only chatted twice but he offered to greet me if I ever visited the theatre or studios where he was working. Later, when in Hollywood, I was taken to the MGM Studios by a scriptwriter friend but, instead of seeing Rex Harrison I watched Greer Garson, Walter Pidgeon and Elizabeth Taylor making the film *Julia Misbehaves*. I was never sure whether or not this was a practical joke on the part of my friend but I congratulated Greer Garson on the uplifting effect she had on all of us during the war with the film *Mrs Miniver*. Generously, she replied, 'But you are not doing so badly yourself, are you?' As Elizabeth Taylor dashed up to her with some flowers, into which was tucked a gold bracelet, to thank her for her help in the film, Greer turned to me and said, 'She's such a sweet child.' Liz Taylor must have been about fourteen years old then.

Years later I was asked by the head of a catering school if I would make some observations on the use of flowers on board these Cunard liners and if I would look into the possibility of training some of the staff on the care of flowers at sea. I was also asked if I would instruct some of the stewards in making a hurried arrangement of flowers, in case a passenger required something special for a party or a dinner table. It appeared that those who thus equipped themselves would be among those chosen to transfer to the new *QE2*. So I did a round trip to New York and back teaching and chatting to the stewards after 10 pm when their duties ceased for the day. I also drew up plans for various methods of arranging, say, two dozen carnations or gladioli, all of which were to be kept in cold store, marking the design with numbers showing where each stem had to be placed. I wrote leaflets on how to keep the flowers alive and on which ones would last longer than others. Although a good deal of information was exchanged, it all had to be stored until the real thing could be put into practice on the new *QE2* which was still on the drawing board.

I am not sure whether the men enjoyed this innovation, but I know I did, and it didn't finish there. In the sixties I was asked if I would advise about the use of plants on board the new ship. I suggested that plants were used almost everywhere but they would have to be of a kind that could withstand the cold Atlantic crossing in winter and the hot balmy cruises in the Caribbean.

I went to Glasgow two or three times and saw this great ocean liner on the blocks during the first stages of construction. I made various measurements, and decided on the number of plants needed, as well as the varieties. Consultation was also necessary with the interior decorators. David Hicks gave me a free hand, Jon Bannenberg wanted no flowers or plants in his room, stating that his own colour schemes would speak for themselves. Michael Inchbald did not mind what was planted as long as the flowers harmonized with his colour scheme in the Queen's Room, which was tastefully decorated in cream, coral and

apple green. Many other plans were made, such as conical arrangements of yellow and orange dried everlasting flowers in gilded urns for
the brown libraries; for the dining tables, little 'trees' of everlasting
flowers, which were to be for breakfast and lunch (lemon table cloths
being used), and pink, cerise and cream 'trees' on pink cloths for dinner,
the centres being lit from beneath. Posy rings of dried and fresh flowers
surrounded other table lamps. One interior decorator wanted only
anemones on his tables in the Britannia Room, without knowing that
they would not be obtainable all year round, so we had to com-
promise.

With my plans for the plants made, I went to my good friend Tom
Rochford, of the House of Rochford, the biggest British grower of
indoor plants at that time and, with his expert advice, a plan was
agreed upon. There were 14 huge planting troughs each 12 feet long
to be filled in the Queen's Room and here, I suggested, in order to
obtain a three-dimensional effect, should be placed the lovely grey-
green *Aechmea fasciata*, with its corally-pink flower head, mixed with
pinky-cream striped dracaena, flanked by *Begonia rex* and peperomias,
interspersed with trailing ivy. At each end of the troughs, height was
regained with *Grevillea robusta*. A favourite plant of mine, *Cissus antarctica*, which is almost indestructible, was agreed upon for the promenade
decks, but the plants had to be ten feet high to start with. These were
to be placed in white fibreglass tubs, the top of the soil being covered
with white pebbles to conserve moisture. They would grow up each
side of the decks joining each other in the centre above.

Although much of this was still only a plan on paper, I sent in my
proposals to those in charge, thinking that by going to the grower I
had saved them a good deal of money. Apparently a single estimate
could not be accepted as the shareholders required this job to be put
out to tender. Mr Rochford then withdrew for, as a wholesale grower,
it was he who would have to supply all the others who might send in
estimates and he could not compete with his own customers. An estimate was finally agreed (much higher than the original one) – so much
for the shareholders. This estimate was then given to a nurseryman in
Scotland as this would save the cost of transport to Glasgow where
the ship was lying in deep water off the Clyde.

The day eventually arrived to do the planting, for the ship was due to make a trial run the next day and everything had to be in order. I went to Glasgow only to find a force-nine gale raging. As I stood on the quayside, it was obvious that no one could board the ship that night. I begged the master of a tug to take me with some of the plants, determined to make a start, and managed with the aid of ropes and a rope ladder to get aboard. But we were not so lucky with the plants, for the tug rose on a very high wave, only to be flung down again continuously. As soon as a plant was handed up, the tug receded and the plant fell into the sea. The lovely aechmeas were awash with sea-water, others were broken off at the tips. With no hope of getting the larger plants aboard that night, the tug returned to port. It made one more attempt but in vain and we had to decide to leave the plant operation until daylight. Although I was only supposed to supervise the planting, there was so much to do that I filled all the troughs with peat and soil and made holes ready to receive the plants in the morning. The ship was due to sail at 10 am, with a complement of staff in order to test all the facilities. That night, I went to bed with my back almost permanently bent but could not sleep as the loudspeakers, delivery trolleys and lifts were being tested all night long.

The gale abated and the next morning the plants were put in place at top speed. The ten-foot-high *Cissus antarctica* stood like sentinels down the promenade deck. The other plants seemed to nod to each other, knowing their places according to size, all were watered and, after saying goodbye to the nurserymen, I was pleased to stagger to the dining-room for a late breakfast. Here I met Lord Mancroft, who kindly invited me to join him on the helicopter that was picking him up just before the ship sailed.

I think the world got to know that the ship developed turbine trouble on this trial run and had to crawl back into Southampton Dock. Here all the plants were eventually taken off and stored in local green-houses for the three months' wait before the ship was ready to sail again.

There were, of course, changes in staff before the official sailing, but I left a chart in each steward's room, giving a coloured picture of each plant, with its common name, then its botanical name, followed with instructions for watering and fertilizing. This was done in case passengers should ask the name of a plant and how they should look after it.

The world-famous *QE2* finally sailed to New York on 2 May 1968 with a full passenger list. Knowing that the ship would be about four days at sea, I sent a telegram to the head steward to greet him on arrival: 'Never you mind about the turbines, just make sure that my plants are watered.' A telegram came back some days later which stated: 'The plants are doing well, but some prefer gin and tonic, others like dry martini.'

It was a great adventure that had a sequel. A few years later, I was travelling to New York on a Pan Am plane when a steward approached me offering me a drink. I looked up and said I did not know Pan Am offered drinks to tourist passengers. He replied that they didn't and that this was on him for, he explained, he was one of the stewards I had instructed in flowers on board the *QE2*.

PART THREE

TAKING ROOT

7

Karachi

I N 1960, I WAS INVITED to visit New Zealand. On my way there, after demonstrating in Italy, I stopped off in Karachi. My plane was delayed but on the tarmac I noticed a petite young woman wearing a pale yellow sari. She was the secretary of the Pakistani Women's Association and was waiting there to meet me. I had been asked by them and the Horticultural Society to talk on flowers, flower shows and flower arranging, to help the women emerge from purdah (so it had been explained to me in letters.)* I was late, and the ladies had been waiting so, leaving my luggage at the airport, I was hurried away by car to the garden of the former mayor of Karachi where the meeting was to be held. There, sitting under a red and gold embroidered canopy, I was introduced to the gathering, all the ladies looking so elegant, dressed in their coloured saris. They seemed relaxed and expectant whilst I seemed hassled, wondering what was expected of me. Then one lady stood up and greeted me. She was most apologetic, explaining that the roses they had obtained for me to work with had all drooped in the heat owing to the delay. I noticed the women had been drinking tea, so I re-cut the stem ends of the roses and stood them in the hot water jug to which I added a couple of teaspoonsful of sugar. I explained that this should revive them.

After a short talk on the principles of design and of using different forms, shapes and sizes of plant material in order to create an interesting picture, I looked around for some examples to illustrate these ideas. The garden was large and, in front of a long wall which surrounded the property, I noticed what seemed like hundreds of tall sansevieria leaves (mother-in-law's tongues). There were huge monstera leaves (sometimes referred to as Swiss cheese plant) growing in abundance and masses of trailing philodendrons, palms, crotons, and a border of caladiums which appeared larger than those we in England treasure as house plants. I asked if I could cut a few of these leaves, which at home I would not dare to do. 'Oh please take what you want,' said the daughter of the house and almost disparagingly added, 'They are only leaves.' So, flourishing my secateurs, I cut masses of them. In one of those beaten-brass Indian bowls, I placed the tall leaves for height. The monsteras then were inserted, some leaning backward, some forward, to give a three-dimensional effect. The trailing philodendron was placed at the side and, lastly, a group of deeper-coloured caladiums was inserted in the centre, to illustrate the principle of using tall, medium and short plant material.

By this time I noticed that the roses had perked up and these, I explained, could be added around the centre for colour interest. We discussed their flower show, which takes place every February, and I promised to send them some dried-flower plaques. The foliage arrangements were transferred to the interior of the house where, I was informed later by letter, they lasted for many weeks. Once inside the house I learned about the work of the Pakistani Women's Association. I was reluctant to leave this gracious house in order to retrieve my luggage for my stay in an hotel.

It seemed strange the next morning, since it was November, to see the gardeners setting out annual seedlings of sweet peas, petunias, Californian poppies and stocks in a geometrical bedding pattern in the surrounds of the hotel.

After sightseeing, the former mayor of Karachi, Mr Sohrab Katrak, in whose garden I had spoken, took me to dinner in the Sind Club. He was fiercely proud of Karachi's connection with England and related the achievements of the British as though they were part of his own work, which I felt certain many of them were. The night was still, ceiling fans swayed, everyone was in evening dress and ladies floated by me wearing beautiful saris. To me, never having been in this part of the world before, it seemed a living picture of what I had imagined life with the Raj to have been. I was spellbound.

We chatted about Pakistan's hopes and fears since partition and through all our conversation ran streams of philosophical wisdom. I posed a question and sat enthralled listening to the answer, especially when I told Mr Katrak what I hoped to achieve with flowers. He was so reassuring. 'You must sit still and tune in,' he said. 'It is all there in the atmosphere – everything is possible.' I was loath to leave for the next stage of my journey to New Zealand and vowed I would return one day for a longer stay. I did not anticipate that my next visit would be of even shorter duration. It happened like this.

In 1963 I had been in Singapore speaking and demonstrating to Air Force wives where I had been sent by my sister-in-law, Lady Tedder. She thought it would be good therapy for me immediately following the death of her brother, Sir Alexander Seton, whom I had married in 1962 and who, six months later, sadly died. For the previous seventeen years I had been alone, devoting my time to my work with flowers and it seemed as though I was meant to go on with this work, alone.

I was in great distress and found it difficult to get up on a platform to try to inspire others when I felt so empty and in despair myself. My audiences all appeared so secure in the sunshine with their husbands, cars and boats, whilst I was so utterly lost. Grief finally overwhelmed me and blinded me to everything other than a need to get home. I needed, also, to talk to someone who might understand my plight. I then thought of Mr Katrak in Karachi and was certain he would console me. So, after cancelling a talk to the Chinese Women's Association, I took a plane out of Singapore that would allow me to stop off anywhere on my way back to London.

There was a three-hour stopover at Karachi so, after having my luggage removed from the plane, thinking I would stay a few days, I telephoned Mr Katrak, not realizing it was only about 2 am. I just told him I was in Karachi and would like to see him. He replied that he would be delighted, then asked if I would phone him in the morning and let him know where I was staying. My spirits were dashed for I needed him at once (how unsure one is in grief). After replacing the telephone shakily, my despair returned and I asked for my baggage to be put back on the plane, explaining that I would continue my flight. I got off the plane again in Cairo where I had spent two previous visits and had friends, but they were not at home, so I continued my journey with a stop in Bahrein, where I had previously spoken to the Air Force wives. Here again the airport was a long way from anyone I knew and the hot winds and sand were blowing fiercely into the open-sided building. I did not know how to make the phone work. It was dark and everyone was so occupied with loading and unloading freight that I was unable to get help. Therefore, as there was only a one-hour stopover, I wandered around the airport looking at the plants, advice on the care of which I had previously given to Royal Air Force personnel. Again I gave up, reaching London on a wet, windy and cold day in February.

In the stillness of my own home, when I had recovered some of my equilibrium, I felt I owed an apology to Mr Katrak for phoning him in the middle of the night and not making contact the next morning as promised. So I wrote to him explaining my grief and what had caused it. He replied with his usual understanding and wisdom stating that in the East, after a death, friends are consoled with philosophical words. He went on to quote several passages from the *Shastra* and *Omar Khayyám* including:

> God will not seek thy race
> Nor will He ask thy birth
> Alone will He demand of thee
> What hast thou done on earth?

Another with cricket as a simile:

> The Ball no Question makes of Ayes and Noes,
> But Right or Left as strikes the Player goes:
> And He that toss'd Thee down into the Field,
> *He* knows about it all – HE knows – HE knows!

Finishing with:

> God marks the span of Life with the birth of a child, and we cannot add even a minute more to the time fixed by Him in His wisdom.

My thoughts of Karachi so often go back to Mr Katrak and the flowers that took me there.

In 1987, at the Second World Flower Arrangement Show held in Brussels, three charming young women dashed up and greeted me

1 An elegant contemporary arrangement, using **flowers** from an English summer garden.

2 A one-to-one hands-on lesson in flower arranging, 1949.

3 A 1950 demonstration to an enthusiastic group in a local hall. Julia is using three blooms on a pin holder in a low dish.

4 Instructing at the first demonstration and judging course at the RHS Halls in London. Many flower arranging pioneers were present.

5 Julia signing copies of her books after a demonstration in Surrey. Audiences were always eager for information and pictures.

6 Ready to depart for the 1954 International Flower Show in New York, fully armed with hat, gloves, and daffodils from Covent Garden.

7 Julia's studio in the Pheasantry, a historic building on the King's Road, Chelsea, in 1960.
Flower groups from home and abroad came here for lessons.

8 Sir Alexander Seton, 10th Baronet of Abercorn, in Seton Chapel, explaining his Coat of Arms to Julia after their marriage in 1962. The Inverness Flower Club staged a reception in their honour.

9 Julia arranged exotic red flowers sent specially from Jamaica for the first
Festival of Flowers in Westminster Abbey, 1966, 'One People'.

10 Off to New York on the *QE2*, 1969. Julia is holding a dried flower 'tree' similar to those placed on each dining table.

lovingly. They were members of the Karachi Floral Art Society. The chairman at that time, Mrs Farida Kalim, told me of the formation of the society in 1967, seven years after my first visit. They were now active, holding monthly meetings, working for charity and organizing the annual flower show, usually held in February. Today, I am happy to hear from their present president, Mrs Sayeed Shahimah, of their work and inwardly feel a sense of gratitude that the seeds I had sown all those years ago have flowered so successfully.

*In the thirty-odd years since I was in Karachi, vast changes have taken place: the women have not only emerged but have also taken their place independently in a fast-moving world.

8
The Wonder of Thailand

I WONDER HOW many recall the motor-racing exploits of Prince Bira of Chakrobongse and his cousin, Prince Chula. Both became great anglophiles after their English education; Prince Chula eventually marrying the fair-haired Elizabeth Hunter, a great friend of mine. It was obvious, therefore, that I should consult him while I was in Thailand to study the flower scene on my way to New Zealand. Prince Chula, a proud erudite man, who so sadly died in 1963 at the age of fifty-five, wrote that revealing book, *The Twains Have Met*.* This describes not only the background of his royal family, but also his romance with his Lisba, which proved a very happy union yet sad, for Lisba died two years after Chula, leaving a baby daughter, Narissa.

On arrival in Bangkok I was met by Pungpit Chulasenok, the wife of Prince Chula's manager and agent who, after installing me in my hotel, took me on a tour of this fairy tale pink-and-white city. First of all, we visited Prince Chula's house. Lisba had not told me of the beauty of the gardens which dipped down to the edge of the river. Tall monstera plants abounded, philodendrons climbed the trees and the huge elephant's ear (*Colocasia*) leaves protruded over the pathways. I was fascinated but I noticed no colour except in the croton leaves. It was only on leaving, when I turned a corner, that I saw a mass of mauve water lilies in a huge pool, floating and moving in the breeze.

Pungpit was very pretty and dainty, as most Thai women are. With hands clasped before her face as though in prayer, she would bow and ask where next I would like to go. Of course it was to see flowers. I was anxious to know how, where and what they grew. Did they use them in the house or on the dining tables? Did they learn about flowers or did their use come naturally? In answer to my many queries Pungpit took me to a domestic-science school where the higher-born young ladies learn social and domestic graces, which include the making of temple flower arrangements. I was introduced on arrival to the Head, a stately woman with sleek black hair, and saw a group of beautiful girls (are there any who are not beautiful in Thailand?) sitting at a round table almost as low as the floor. I watched carefully as they worked, so let me explain how these conical shapes for the temples are created. First, a brass bowl is filled with wet sawdust. Next, a ring of small flowers is placed, heads outwards, over the rim with the stems pointing inwards. These are held down with another layer of wet sawdust, which is followed by another ring of flowers, each layer becoming smaller in circumference until the top of the cone-shape is reached. Here a small bunch of flowers is inserted. The more advanced pupils alternate the colours of flowers used, inserting perhaps three red, four green, two white, and so on, something like the Fair Isle knitting that is practised in Scotland.

Our next stop was at a marble temple to see the Golden Buddha and I was delighted to see about twenty of the cone-shaped flower designs of varying sizes. I looked closely and it seemed that they were made of the everlasting flower *Gnaphalium*. Some of the cones had dried, giving the appearance of parchment, others were bright and colourful, obviously just freshly made. I asked if these were placed in the temple on special days, say on Sundays, and was told that there was no day such as our Sunday, each week. Their religious days were twice a month, changing with the moon.

Many of the private houses I saw were on stilts with open sides. Shoes were removed at the top of the steps as the floors were highly polished. Exquisitely carved tables, about six inches high off the ground, were placed in front of low settees banked with brightly coloured cushions. I was taken to one such house, the home of Mr and Mrs Jahavicharara, whose daughter was training at the Sadler's Wells Ballet School in London. Mr Jahavicharara was an amateur orchid grower and gave me several sprays for my hotel room. I noticed, on one low table, sprays of *Philodendron scandens* held down with stones in a shallow glass dish in which stood a wood carving of a heron – so simple yet so effective. In the centre of the open-sided house was a closed-in raised platform. I assumed this was where the kitchen and bedrooms were situated.

On leaving, Mrs Jahavicharara gave me a head of *Donya aurora*, a flower that looks like a large white rhododendron. Purple and cerise bougainvillea and red and orange cannas seemed to flourish everywhere and were vying with the colourful dresses of the ladies.

Tall flowers for cutting did not seem to be available, but single florets of cannas, sometimes hibiscus, were often threaded onto a thin strip of bamboo. Sadly, they only last a day. At a dinner I noticed single hibiscus flowers spread on the table in a serpentine pattern. The alternate pink and crimson flowers gave a delightful effect and, on enquiry, Pungpit told me that hibiscus flowers, picked in bud, were kept in the refrigerator until nearing dinner time when they were brought out and placed on the table. The effect, as I saw it, was magical as they burst open in the warmth of the room.

I visited a wonderful garden designed by its owner, Mr Udom Buranasiri, an architect at Chulalonghorn University. His skill was noticeable in the winding paths that led to various vistas but it was the sight of dieffenbachias, nine feet high, that caught my eye as well as an eight-foot, hedge-like effect of crested euphorbias. I thought back to the struggle I have at home in trying to keep my dieffenbachia alive and healthy in winter in my dry, heated rooms. Here it was moist and, although the temperature was 85°F (29°C), I was told it was the beginning of their cool season.

I was fortunate to be in Bangkok at the time of the Great Exhibition celebrating the city as it was fifty years ago. Bangkok, of course, is not an ancient city, only about two hundred years old, but here they exhibited styles of dress, music, dancing and all kinds of crafts which were practised many years ago. I could not be torn away from the flower-craft stands. Here I saw young girls making the most intricate bracelets, necklaces, earrings, hair ornaments and garlands, from various small flowers positioned with a needle on to thread. What particularly took my eye were the single flowers of the heavily scented pinky-white tuberose, a bracelet of which was made for me. I was told that few girls would go out without wearing some form of flower ornamentation.

I later gave some demonstration lessons in the English style of arrangements for dining tables and for special occasions, which fascinated the Thais. They sat in silence watching me just as I had previously been intrigued watching them gently place an orchid in position with such great care and tenderness.

Still vivid in my mind, I remember the brightly painted temples and the icing effect of the pink, white and pale green buildings, all making Bangkok the most colourful city in the world. The canals by the sides of the roads were full of water lilies, the oxygenating weeds keeping the water clean. Everyone smiled and everyone seemed trusting.

I recall the time when it was obvious I would have to see a doctor at the hospital to treat the mosquito bites that I had suffered through stupidly walking through long grass at dusk. After examination I was given a prescription, the medicine to be picked up at the exit. There I was charged a certain amount but, as I had no money with me, the nurse said she would pay as she had to close her books each day, and added that I could bring the money the next day.

Feeling better in the morning I went sightseeing and it was not until two days later that I returned with the money. She put her hands together in the customary style, smiled and said: 'Thank you, I knew you would return.' On another occasion, I called a taxi one evening from my hotel and asked to be taken to the Theatre of Thai Dancing. A smiling driver arrived and, on depositing me at the entrance to the theatre, I asked the cost of the fare. He smiled, then asked if I was going back to the hotel after the performance. I replied that I was. 'Then you don't pay now, I will wait for you.' I thought he was taking a risk, for all the men looked the same to me and I might have taken another taxi but, as I emerged later and stood on the steps, this driver came forward calling: 'Missy, Missy, I come back to take you to the hotel.' Can you imagine this happening in London or New York? It was this sense of trust that made a lasting impression on me. It endeared me to the Thais and I left with the feeling that if their behaviour was the manifestation of Buddhism, their country's religion or their way of life, then perhaps it should be studied more and put into practice by us all.

*Published by Foulis in 1956

9

New Zealand and Fiji

I HAD ALREADY been travelling for more than a month in 1960 and now I was approaching New Zealand, my first visit to that wonderful country. As I neared my destination I began to wonder what these people might expect of me. Was I adequate? For I faced a very heavy programme of twenty-four demonstrations in different towns in the month I was to be there.

I have, however, as I became more experienced, learned to turn my attention outwards, away from myself, so instead of worrying about the hall, the flowers and what they might expect of me, I decided to explain to my audience that I was an ordinary woman who just wanted to tell them what pleasures and self-expression could be gained through the art of flower arranging. I could not foresee the questions that might be asked, so I decided to work only in the present, meeting everything as it came and, if I trusted, I felt I would be helped, for basically I knew my subject.

But why was I going to New Zealand in the first place? There was to be an important Rose Festival in the sulphur-spring town of Rotorua to promote it as a resort. There was also to be a national show and other activities with flower-arrangement classes and I had been invited to open the show, to judge and to demonstrate.

At that time in New Zealand there were no flower clubs (as we know them today), but there were many horticultural societies with floral-art sections. The professional florists, who were very good, seemed to do most of the teaching when needed.

As I contemplated the proposed programme, I was aware that it would be an exhausting trip for, not only would I have to take a very early plane each day to reach my destination, but I was also scheduled to meet the local press and radio, and the mayor, in addition to organizing the venue or, at least, overseeing it. Then there were the flowers to be found and receptions by the committee to be attended at every stage. I acknowledged, however, that I could only take one step at a time and that I must do my best at each step, rather than think of the many engagements before me. There was always a social evening after the demonstration and I would eventually fall into bed, well after midnight, to rise again at 6 am for my next flight.

The enthusiasm was great everywhere I demonstrated. In one town the shops were decorated for my visit, in another flags were out, and in yet another I was given a blessing by the vicar when a church service was given especially for me. The audiences were great, between 500 and 700; sometimes, in theatres, there would be as many as 1,800 people. I am not sure if they were all interested in flower arranging but my message of learning to strike out and to believe in oneself, even to starting flower clubs as self-expression, was simple. More information was requested and, on my return home, I sent out leaflets on 'How To Form a Club', and 'Hints for Judges' as well as books. In places such as Christchurch, Auckland, Nelson, Wellington, Plymouth, Gisborne and Dunedin, people crowded into the halls, and I became more and more fascinated with this lovely country.

As I flew from place to place I was able to look down on the indented coastline fringed with sandy beaches. Previously I had no idea that New Zealand was so attractive topographically. Each day I took a different type of plane, sometimes an eight-seater, sometimes a sixteen-seater and, once or twice, it was just me and the pilot in a small plane flying over fields, trees and rooftops. The mountains were impressive and the winding rivers – there are twenty-six alone that run into Lake Taupo – are well stocked with trout for which anyone can fish on payment of a small licence fee to the government.

On a few occasions I travelled by road and it seemed that everyone had a small garden, planned around a bungalow. There were few people or cars on the country roads (no stops for 'Teas Served Here'). I noticed the lovely yellow wild lupins and wild arum lilies growing in abundance by the roadside or in the ditches. I saw *Leucospermum cordifolium* growing for the first time and, in abundance, the cabbage tree (*Cordyline australis*) with its white flowers, which was so called because the early settlers ate the crowns as a substitute for cabbage. Wild flowers abounded and I presented the prizes at an exhibition of native wild-flower arrangements at which the members of the society had not only to name all the flowers used, but also to fashion their container from wild or natural plant materials. It was a delightful exhibition at the end of which I was presented with a wild-flower bouquet. The next morning, remembering my New York experience with Princess Elizabeth's orchid, I bought some powdered borax, and filled a shoe box in which I buried the bouquet, and sent it to England where it remained, preserved, on show in my studio for a number of years.

The hills in the countryside, often covered with sheep, seemed to rise straight up from the roadside where manuka bushes, which look like a flowering broom, also grew in abundance. This bush, I learned later, is commonly called a tea tree, for early settlers used to dry the small leaves and seed heads and pour boiling water over them, to make a brown concoction which they called 'tea'.

Everything was new to me, as well as to the organizers. Although I would send in advance a list of flowers I would need, I could only ever quote the usual market varieties as I did not know what else might be available. In the end, kind ladies came to my assistance and either brought me flowers and plants or told me where they could be found. I only had to ask – a simple measure which I could have learned after my first day. I should, perhaps, have arrived a few days earlier to get acclimatized to the country and to eventual situations. But it was early days in the floral-art scene and I have learned since.

Hurrying to some of the gardens, I noticed how neat and tidy they all were, with flowers similar in variety to ours in England but seemingly much larger, probably owing to more months of sunshine. My hosts, twenty-two of them, all connected with horticulture in some way, extended themselves to help me. I wish I could meet them all again in less hurried circumstances.

There was little time for leisure or exciting adventures, for it was a working tour, but I can now look back on one particular event which I tell against myself. During a short air trip, I sat next to a gentleman and, in chatting, I told him I thought New Zealand was a marvellous country. I continued to extol its virtues, he nodding his assent now and again. As we landed he held back and told me to go ahead, so after bidding him goodbye I descended to the tarmac only to spot about eight or more photographers, jockeying for position. Surely, I thought to myself, the flower people cannot think I am all that important. I smilingly walked towards the photographers and as I did so they dodged from right to left to avoid me. Looking behind me, I saw the object of their attention was the man I had sat next to. He was Sir Walter Nash, the prime minister of New Zealand, and I had been selling his country to him.

I had a crowded audience and the next morning the newspapers reported that the political meeting was not as well attended as was expected due to a flower-arranging demonstration held in the town at the same time.

As I write I recall another touch I admired. It was the way the bridges over the roadways were planted both sides with colourful trailing geraniums and other plants – they seemed to be hanging from the brickwork. Everywhere I went I took note of more and more indigenous plants, all of which I hoped would increase my horticultural knowledge.

I have often wondered at the end of a tour if any lasting impressions have been made and if anything permanent will result from a visit. Alone at night in someone's guest room or an hotel 12,000 miles from home, I would ask myself why I was there; I was no one in particular, I had no great knowledge to impart and I did not consider myself an entertainer with flowers. Rather by speaking and demonstrating I wanted to pass on to others the art of arranging flowers, to inspire them, to uncover latent ability. I spoke of my own simple start and encouraged others to begin likewise.

So it was gratifying to learn from Mrs Mary MacKay, who was president at the time of writing, that in 1965 the Floral Art Society of New Zealand was formed. Due to the enthusiasm of the pioneers, and I recall Mrs Barbara Cave, it now has 111 affiliated groups with 4,000 members. I hear often of their activities and applaud all they do for charity; I am also sent pictures of their exhibits at shows which reveal a high standard of artistry. I smiled when I heard recently that they had flown out from Britain a young man to give one demonstration at one of their conferences; 12,000 miles for one appearance. The early days of 24 demonstrations in 28 days are past. They are now fully established.

New Zealand is a paradise for many reasons. On my trip, it was very rewarding horticulturally, and topographically it was beyond my expectations. I shall also never forget the people who wave the British flag more vigorously than we in Britain do ourselves. I shall always be grateful for the flowers that gave me the opportunity of going there. If only New Zealand were not so far away. They will be the host country for the World Show in 1996.

One thousand, three hundred miles north of New Zealand in the South Pacific Ocean lies the island of Fiji. When I visited in 1984, I was greeted by a flower garland and Mrs Maureen Strickland telling me how happy she was to see me, as they planned all their shows by my books. I was flattered and delighted to be welcomed so warmly in Suva, the capital of this lovely island, where ginger flowers, heliconias and orchids flourish so plentifully. In her garden I had to duck my head to walk under arbours cascading with heavy blooms of lobster-claw heliconia, contrasting with the bunches of delicate laburnum and wistaria that form similar archways in our gardens in England.

Until a short while before my visit, Mrs Strickland had been the president of the floral art group of the horticultural society, the members meeting once monthly to discuss plants and flowers and how best to use them. An arrangement of about twenty red ginger flowers combined with light green papyrus and centred low down with the lobster-claw heliconia was a sight I did not expect to see at their meeting; with such exotic material available I would have been happy to use just two or three stems, with some of their sword-like pendanus leaves, in a modern design. I might have added one or two pink pineapples (*Ananas comosus* 'Variegatus'), which grows on long stems striking out from the striped leaves in the centre of the plant.

It was the foliage in Fiji that amazed me even more than the flowers, for I saw dracaena and maranta leaves growing out of doors in abundance. We in England would guard them preciously as house plants. The three-legged wooden bowls, carved in one piece from the local dakua tree, also attracted me, for I could see their potential use in modern designs. Although sugar is one of the island's main industries and ginger and coconut are good sources of export, I felt that if only some of their plant material could be exported flower arrangers in the rest of the world would leap at the chance of using it.

Flower arrangers are keen and active in Fiji; Mrs Strickland told me that they had decorated the National Stadium for the Queen's visit in 1982, on the occasion of the dedication ceremony for religious leaders. The Queen must have found the sight of these colourful exotic flowers in such abundance unforgettable.

10

Australia and Hong Kong

BEFORE I set out for New Zealand in 1960, I had sat next to an astrologer at a 'Woman of the Year' luncheon. I mentioned my proposed visit and asked her if it was a good time to go. We exchanged addresses and I gave her my time and date of birth and other details she needed. Later she wrote to me stating that New Zealand would be good for me at the time I was intending to go but, she added, do not attempt Australia: wait for two or three years when it will be much more successful for you there. I did not take much notice, for Australia was not on my programme at that time. However, flushed with the successful tour of New Zealand, I *did* phone my contacts and went on to Australia.

The Australian Broadcasting Station had arranged a coast-to-coast interview, but alas my plane was two hours late so this was cancelled. Just after my arrival in Sydney it rained — then it blew gales and it continued to rain incessantly for three days. I was told this was unusual but it did prevent me from stepping out to visit gardens or to see the sights. So I phoned my good friend Paul Jones, the world-renowned artist of flowers and plants, and he dropped his painting to drive me around the various bays and waterways. Paul has exhibited his painting all over the world. In London I had seen his large work on the jade vine (*Strongylodon macrobotrys*) with its long, green-blue pendant racemes of flowers against a dark jungle-like background. It was breathtaking. I wonder who owns it now?

Paul pointed out various spots of interest as we drove around the bays and beaches but I could hardly see anything except wattle trees* between the constant swish of the flashing windscreen wipers. Luckily Professor Waterhouse, the great expert on camellias, was at home so we drove to see his Japanese teahouse and garden. I enjoyed our chat in his peaceful home surrounded by Mrs Waterhouse's beautiful flower arrangements in the oriental style.

Rain rather discolours one's view of a city and I am afraid it did mine of Sydney, but I was cheered when I met the members of the Royal Horticultural Society of New South Wales to whom I gave a talk. I also attended their Christmas party and exhibition of flower arrangements, which were mostly in the mass style, featuring gladioli, ti leaves, (*Cordyline terminalis*), bottlebrush flowers (*Callistemon*) and frangipani, it being summer, despite the rain. They then drove me to the famous Bondi Beach where we had dinner and talked about flowers well into the night.

Woman's Day magazine phoned me and plans were made for competitions and demonstrations in two years' time, when it was arranged that I should return. The rain cleared and everyone seemed happy and light-hearted as they hurried about their business, but I was booked on a plane to Adelaide where I was due to judge a show. I stopped overnight in Melbourne to visit Dr Thomas, the famous rosarian and president of the Australian Rose Society. The sun shone brightly in Melbourne and, with my spirits lifted, the Thomases took me on a tour of the city and parks. In the landscaped Botanical Gardens I was intrigued to see, for the first time, great bushes of green and red kangaroo-paw (*Anigozanthos flavidus*), so called for its felted, hairy flowers shaped like paws. I enjoyed Melbourne.

I flew on to Adelaide where I had agreed to open and judge their flower show. Here the temperature was 98°F (36°C). My hostess, Mrs Greta Lance Lewis, was busy staging the flower show so, unable to be with her (as a judge must not be present during staging) and it being too hot to walk out, I sat in a darkened room with the shutters closed to keep out the flies. Was the astrologer correct? I wondered, for I had dreamed of sitting on the beach.

The next day I found the show was excellent, the Christmas exhibits being particularly original but the attendance suffered due to the excessive heat which rose daily. It was 22 December and I felt that to stage a show so near Christmas for my benefit was a courageous effort. I was indebted to all the exhibitors who had worked so hard and I made many friends with whom I am still in touch. Everyone was friendly and enthusiastic and I am sure Adelaide had much to offer, but the heat was too much for me. I therefore decided to move on, via Hong Kong, to my engagements in Japan.

I arrived in Hong Kong where I was to spend Christmas, helping with
the flowers at the YWCA. Almost before I had unpacked I went out to
look at the shops, all brilliantly lit with glittering goods. As I was
staring into a window, a fresh-faced young man with an American
accent said: 'Aren't all the things exciting here?' 'Yes,' I replied and
made way to move on. He then said his friend was inside buying
something for his mother and explained that they were missionaries
and could only move in pairs. His friend emerged from the shop and,
noticing that we were chatting, asked if I would join them for dinner. I
hesitated, but he explained that his mother had sent him a hundred
dollars to take some lonely person to dinner. I wasn't lonely, but I was
alone and it was Christmas Eve. When they said they would have to
hurry, as they had to be back at the mission by 9 pm, I accepted.

We had a meal and exchanged cards, and the next morning I
arranged some flowers in their mission. I thought that would be the
end of the encounter, so I was surprised some months later at home to
receive a letter from a lady in Illinois saying she was pleased that her
young son had picked me for a dinner companion, for she possessed
most of my books and had been in the audience when I had spoken to
her garden club. The world is often a very small place.

There were no flower clubs in Hong Kong at that time, but today
the Hong Kong Flower Club, started in 1979, is highly successful. Mrs
Jenni Bewick, the president at the time of writing, tells me that they
invite demonstrators and teachers from England and hold shows; these
in turn support charities and, in particular, children's needs at the John F
Kennedy Centre where five or six members go each month to teach
handicapped children flower arranging. The club supplies the flowers
up to a cost of HK$250 (about £23.00 at the time of writing). The
children keep the flowers. I thoroughly support this positive example
of members becoming involved in helping others.

On looking back, remembering the rain and then the heat, I feel I
should have heeded the astrologer's warning that Australia was not for
me at the time of my first visit in 1960.

However, in 1984 I made a return trip and, oh, what a difference! It
was a February, the weather was perfect, the city of Sydney seemed to

glitter and the Opera House visit was unforgettable. The 741-acre Royal Botanical Gardens, with their imposing Woollomooloo Gates, was a great surprise to me, not only for the sub-tropical plant material but also for the statues and scenic effects provided by the surrounding water. I love to see statues in large gardens as they break up the constant green of the trees and shrubs and introduce a different form. A happy and vigorous land is Australia, where opportunities abound, provided you have something to give, and where the sun always shines – except for those four days I spent there earlier in the rain.

This time I was able also to make closer contact with the Royal Horticultural Society of New South Wales. Mrs Jean Slattery, the secretary, described their annual Festival of Flowers held in September at St Andrew's, Sydney, the oldest cathedral in Australia; but my visit being in February I was unable to see this spectacular event for myself.

Most of the metropolitan suburbs, and towns in the country areas, have floral-art groups and clubs, many of which are affiliated to the Royal Horticultural Society. Also each state has a state body, delegates from which attend meetings of the Australian Association of Floral Art Judges.

I was unable to get to Perth where I had hoped to see the vast stretches of wild flowers. Mrs Ann Packer, of the West Australian Floral Art Society, later told me the best time would be between August and October. She also told me they felt a little isolated in flower-arranging activities being 3,000 miles away from Sydney but now, since the formation of the Australian National Association, the states have become closer and there is a better exchange of ideas.

Mrs M Mysers of the Garden Club of Australia gave me a great deal of information about their activities which vary according to the plant material in the different climates of that vast country. There are clubs in the Northern Territories and judges' schools in South Australia – 2,500 miles apart. The interest is growing; floral art having proved to be an expressive outlet for so many people. The shows are well attended and a lot is being done for charity.

Although I was impressed by much I saw, it was the Sydney Opera House that left the deepest mark on my mind. I have seen many edifices that have stirred me deeply but this unusual building represented the future, and at every step I took, whether it was outside or inside the building, I was forced to stand and stare. It was stunning. My journey here had been about flowers but there was so much more to experience: the people, the vigour, the life, the sun-bronzed bodies in Sydney and the signs at every corner which read 'To the Beaches', made me think how lucky are these Australians to be part of a throbbing city, yet to be so near to the many water inlets and the open sea.

*The prolific wattle trees were so named because they were used by early settlers in Australia as 'wattle daub': walls were made by interweaving the leafy branches, then covering them with mud. The tree is really acacia, which we in the West call mimosa.

11

Japan and Hawaii

ON ARRIVING at Tokyo airport from Hong Kong after Christmas in 1960, the first thing I noticed was a huge display of what looked like tangled branches, some upside down, with chrysanthemums tucked in here and there, plus a lobster, or what I thought must be the shell of a lobster, in the centre. I was later to discover that a lobster is symbolic of longevity and is used in New Year arrangements as a symbol of long life and happiness. The display stood in a bed of white stone chips surrounded by bricks.

On the long drive from the airport to my hotel, there were tall groupings of pine branches, plum blossom and yew all tied together with straw or red and white ribbons outside every house. These were also New Year decorations, just as we might hang greenery on front doors at Christmas time; the red and white ribbons denoting celebration. I was excited, my eyes taking in every little detail as we drove along. There was a flower arrangement similar to the one at the airport in the reception hall of the hotel.

I was in Japan by invitation to look at the flower-arranging scene and, at the same time, to take lessons from the fountain head. I should use the word 'heads' for I had booked myself in at all three main schools. It was six days before New Year's Day as I had arrived earlier than originally planned due to Australia's heat and I had forgotten that New Year was such an important celebration in the Japanese calendar.

However, anxious to establish myself at the school, I made my way the next day to the imposing Sogetsu building where I was told that the place was closed for New Year. I saw a number of ladies arriving with their bundles of flowers, scissors, and other impedimenta, all tied up in a cloth or *furoshiki*. On asking what they were going to do, I was told they were coming for lessons. 'But you told me you were closed,' I remarked. 'Yes, we *are* closed,' the receptionist answered. This was my first taste of the many paradoxes one meets in Japan. When I explained I was from England and had received confirmation of my lessons from the head master, I was told to come again in the New Year. We were obviously not communicating very well.

Everything seemed to close down for about six days but there were crowds, dressed in their best kimonos, making their way en masse to the Meiji shrine, where they all threw coins across the barrier. I followed and did the same. Small children, wearing their colourful costumes, with twinkling ornaments in their hair, ran joyfully between parents and friends, and the young grownups could be seen along the crowded route carefully posing for photographs. It was all very interesting but my mind was on the cost of the hotel whilst waiting six days for my lessons; in the end I decided to go sightseeing.

After visiting Nikko (two hours by fast train out of Tokyo) where the great 310-foot-high waterfall was frozen solid, and a visit (all too short) to the Stone Garden in Kyoto, which was much smaller than I had imagined, and taking part in a tea ceremony, I was pleased to accept an invitation to dinner with a Japanese flower-arranging friend whom I had met in London, and made my way to her home by taxi. This was not easy as the streets were unnamed and the houses not numbered. The taxi driver always expects *you* to know where your destination is. Fortunately, I had been given a map. It was New Year's Eve and I was greeted by my friend dressed in a beautiful red and gold kimono, her husband, his mother and two children. I saw a delicate linear-style flower arrangement in the *tokonomo* (a large recess seen in most traditional Japanese homes), which seemed somehow 'born' and not made. This was accompanied by a hanging scroll, which I stood and stared at for some while before speaking. We eventually sat down on cushions before the low table which was covered with all kinds of culinary delights. Visual appearance is very important in Japanese cooking and, before me, I noticed a great variety of colourful dishes: some looked like blancmange; others were oblong pieces of solid rice (I suppose made with gelatine) on which a strip of fish rested; various items were sculptured into fantastic shapes, topped with what looked like smoked salmon, then glazed. I imagined these were the hors d'oeuvres, but so many were passed around and placed before me that

I began to think they composed the main meal. But there was more to come. The Japanese like everything freshly cooked so, to cut down the time between kitchen and table, a hot plate on which a pan is placed and in which small slithers of raw meat and vegetables are lightly cooked, is often put in the middle of the table. My friends told me that food tastes better if eaten with wooden chopsticks but these I could not manage. It is said that in Japan about a hundred million pairs of chopsticks are used and thrown away each day. I enjoyed my evening but on the whole I found Japanese food rather bland, and did not enjoy the raw fish; but *flowers*, and not food, were my main concern.

Two days later I presented myself again at the school to check my dates of entry, and found that they could take me right away in a group lesson on New Year celebration arrangements. I hurriedly took my place and the head master announced that red was the colour for celebration. Then, having been told I was from England, he came to me and said: 'In Japan everything must be natural, we are very interested in nature and we only use flowers in season.' This was another paradox for outside the bare tree branches were wired down, covering the cages placed there to create different shapes. Most of the branches used in flower arranging were cut, or tied or twisted or wedged, to suit the style, which seemed to me most *un*natural. Nevertheless, it was not for me to voice these observations, so I went with the others to the flower room. I chose a branch of plum blossom, some pine and three red carnations. (I presumed this blossom was *Prunus subhirtella* 'Autumnalis', which flowers in England from November to March.) I made my arrangement fairly quickly for I really wanted to watch the others at work. I then spotted a dear little Japanese lady in an attractive cream and gold silk kimono making an arrangement of yellow roses. As the colour red had been suggested for celebration I asked why the lady was using *yellow* roses. The master then bowed and explained that 'yellow was nice with pine'. Not being satisfied with that answer and remembering that he said they use only flowers in season, and it being freezing outside, I said: 'But they are roses and you said we must use only flowers in season.' He bowed again and said, with a broad smile and in a lilting voice: 'Yes, roses in season, we buy them this morning.' And so I bowed, and still perplexed said

'Thank you,' realizing that his idea of seasonal flowers and mine were seasons apart. I became aware much later that many seeming paradoxes arose through a lack of communication as, for instance, when a teacher told me the first stem must 'go up', then, the next day when I asked if I could repeat the procedure, he told me the first stem must 'go down'. I reminded him that yesterday he had told me the first stem must go up. He then bowed and smiled saying, but that was yesterday. All this came about because we did not understand each other. I am sure there was a good explanation for what might be considered deliberately misleading. He might have thought that on the second day, I'd asked for a different arrangement. It was very confusing, especially as this was my first visit to Japan.

I recall whilst waiting for this teacher to return from the market that I glanced down at his garden. It was a gem, only about 18 feet by 12 but it represented an exquisite picture in various shades of green. There was a small pool in which stood a bronze heron at the edge of which was a moss-covered stone lantern. Pale green Japanese acers swerved over the pool whilst iris and ferns covered the banks held up by wooden logs. Taller trees such as pine, camellia and pieris seemed to form the background to screen this peaceful oasis from its neighbour. This screening seems not to be as difficult as in England, for the houses are crowded together like jigsaw puzzles, some forwards others backwards. Symmetry is anathema to the Japanese, only assymmetry is beautiful. It was difficult to turn from this little scene to the business of having lessons.

It was only after leaving Japan when I read the book *The Chrysanthemum and the Sword* by Ruth Benedict*, an anthropologist, that many of my misconceptions were clarified. Misunderstandings happened all the time. For instance, when visiting a temple I saw lots of small pieces of paper twisted onto the branches of the bare tree outside where a fortune teller usually sat. I asked my guide the reason for this and he explained that if you have your fortune told, it is written on a piece of paper. If it is bad you put it on the tree and 'woof' comes the wind and blows it away. If it is good, you place it in your pocket.

I could not wait to have my fortune told and when it was translated it appeared that it was good so, with a questioning look and an agreeing nod from my guide, I placed it in my pocket. After touring the shrine and exiting by another door, I saw a different fortune teller and, wishing to get my story right, I said to my guide, 'I keep mine in my pocket, yes, and not on tree?' He replied, 'Yes, but you can put good ones also on tree and "woof" comes the wind and makes it better.' It is this use of 'yes' and 'no' that one meets in Japan that makes for so many difficulties and which explains why an American friend told me that it is no use learning the word 'no' in the Japanese language, for no self-respecting Japanese would ever use it. It would be politely forced on *you* to mention the negative, whilst he would agree with a 'yes'. To clarify this further she said: 'They will smile and say "yes" when they really mean "no", the "yes" meaning "Yes, I hear you".'

I enjoyed my stay, spending my time between lessons at the Sogetsu School, also with Mr Houn O'Hara, a head master, and a charming young lady of the Ikenobo School, who came to my hotel each day to give me more lessons. Mr O'Hara, head of his famous school, whom I came to admire tremendously, invited me to his prizewinning ceremony. Here I was surprised to see the important people sitting at the back whilst the younger students were in the front. Was this a sign of humility or the 'non-claiming' theory of Eastern philosophy? Of course it might have been that the students were placed nearer to the front for quicker and easier accessibility to the prizegiving platform. I began to wonder if I were not 'seeing' more things than I need in every situation. I was asked to speak at the dinner and, through an interpreter, I said I hoped they would pursue and pass on by example to others their simple meditative style of Heaven, Man and Earth rather than follow the confused styles I had seen at exhibitions, in which twisted wire, bent iron, old wheels and upside-down flowers were used to gain effect.

One Japanese lady told me that she did not 'see' anything in our mixed summer groups of flowers. 'They look confused,' she added. Of course we in Britain often enjoy a mixed group of summer flowers and look upon them as the result of horticultural skill placed with taste. I explained I did not 'see' anything in these more modern Japanese styles which seemed so cluttered that I could not give credence to their being likened to anything.

With the help of books and some basic lessons on one of my early

American trips, I was somewhat conversant with the Japanese flower scene before I arrived, but I was surprised at the great number of schools (there are some 3,000 now) and the enormous number of students of flower arranging that exist there. It seems that everyone, both men and women, learn flower arranging and their study continues for many years. It is not considered a domestic subject, an aspect of decorating the home, as it is in the West, but is accepted more as a symbolic art form, a philosophical subject, which encourages awareness of the flowers and plants that are used. This awareness is seen also in the wrappings of a parcel or the tying of string, all of which are considered art forms. Pinpointing the mind on the task in front of one seems to come perhaps from the teaching of Buddha (Buddhism, with Shinto, being the main religion taught in Japan) and this meditative approach is evident in the older generation. I did notice a change among the young who seem to want to forge ahead much more quickly and are far more competitive. Often the older people tend to remain silent when meeting strangers, and one might easily fall into the trap of filling this space with empty chat. The Japanese, however, often judge you by what you do *not* say rather than what you do.

Some factories and offices have breaks for flower arranging, and such times would be used as therapy. I recall visiting a large store to meet a man to whom I had an introduction, but on enquiring was told he had gone to flower arranging and would be back in half an hour. It was then 11 am.

A Westerner arriving in Japan for the first time is often very surprised to find that things are not what he or she had imagined, just as I am sure we in the West must present a strange picture to our Japanese friends. It is better not to have a preconceived view, for it will all be enjoyed so much more if the mind is left open and receptive. For instance, I had imagined (it was 1960) that I would see dainty young women, looking very feminine, shuffling along in their colourful kimonos, with all the time there is to spare. It was not like that with the young teacher, who came to my hotel during her lunch hour wearing a short skirt. After a busy morning at work she would arrive breathless, after parking her baby in a nursery school, only to leave me after an hour to go on elsewhere. Nevertheless, there is an atmosphere of gentle politeness everywhere and a great respect for the elderly – and not only the elderly, but also for one's superiors. I recall, when meeting one of the top masters for the first time, that I bowed. He, having been told I was a master in England, bowed much lower in respect. I, conscious that in Japan he was the more important, then bowed lower still, only to notice in return he went even lower. Nearing the ground, I gave up and we smiled in agreement. All this seems to contrast with the brutalities perpetrated during the war, but it can be better understood after reading *The Chrysanthemum and the Sword*. The book explains that each individual is responsible to the one above *him* and so on, which, as far as I could see, leaves the individual at the bottom of the hierarchy with no freedom other than to obey a rule or command. This system can be observed in families, where the head of the family makes all the decisions and, although there may be a grown-up son with a family of his own, he is still obedient to his father and cannot take charge until his father announces his retirement or dies.

The same approach is recognizable in the schools of flower arranging where each student is responsible to her teacher and that teacher is responsible to the one who taught *her* and that particular teacher is responsible to the one above *her* (all of a different grade, the attainment of each grade certificate costing more money), and each teacher promising to perpetuate the school.

When you know that there are 40,000 teachers in Tokyo city alone and that there are branches with thousands of teachers with students all over the world, it is not difficult to understand why the main schools have such imposing premises and the head masters are so wealthy.

I have often been asked about the significant difference between the Japanese style of arranging flowers and the Western style. It is difficult to answer in a few words, and I can only generalize, but as I see it, the Japanese way embodies more symbolism – the arranger would see something in her arrangement or there would be a meaning expressed. The linear three-dimensional patterns are clearly viewed against the bare walls of the *tokonomo*, very little furniture is visible in the home, and most possessions are tucked away in cupboards; whereas in England we exhibit our possessions, and a profusion of flowers is usu-

ally seen in the more traditional homes against a background of pictures, ornaments and furniture. A three-dimensional linear pattern in
these circumstances would be lost. Again, in Britain, the flowers are
looked upon as the product of the grower's skill and the arranger's
artistry; the more rare and perfect the flowers or plants, the greater the
knowledge of the gardener. In Japan, plants would be used in all stages
of growth. Even if the leaves are bent or riddled with insect holes, it is
all part of nature in their thinking, whereas we would discard a leaf if it
were not perfect, as it would suggest bad cultivation. An advanced
flower arranger in Japan might add a leaf swerving downwards, it
being understood to be a dew-dropping leaf, and insert another
upwards as a dew-catching leaf; whereas we in the West would want
to know what the leaf was, when to plant it and what soil it might
require. So, in brief, one is symbolic and the other horticultural; but on
both counts, the subject is a long and fascinating one.

During my four-week stay in Japan, studying at various schools,
attending shows and exhibitions, I fell victim to a most virulent cold
which I could not shake off. So, on leaving Tokyo bound for Los
Angeles, I stopped off in Hawaii for a few days.

Arriving at 2 am I found my hotel room spacious and welcoming
with a bowl of fruit on the table into which was tucked an orchid. The
verandah windows were open, the air was warm and balmy, and it
seemed just what I needed to cure my cold. As I looked out I could see
the water gently lapping on the soft sand over which the palm trees
swayed in the breeze. It was all too good to be missed. I did not want
to go to bed, so I went down to the beach, took off my shoes and
walked barefoot for an hour along the sandy beach. I then slept well
and my cold vanished.

With flowers still on my mind, the next day I went to watch the
attractive garlands, called leis (pronounced 'lays'), being made. In addition to the various flowers used, such as bougainvillea, stephanotis,
tuberose, oleander, ixora, pakalana, vine flowers, and many others
picked from the colourful South Pacific trees, I was surprised to see the
number of different styles in which these leis were made: some were
single, some round, others double and some were created in what they

call the Maunaloa style, which comprises a knot in the string between each flower. The girls work very quickly, threading about twenty-four flower heads onto needles before sliding them down the string. The lei needles come in different lengths, rather like very long darning needles, which hold the string or thick cotton onto which the flower heads are threaded. I bought a needle thinking I might practise the art at home but other demands have been more pressing.

I hated leaving this warm, sunny country and I can understand why the Waikiki Beach with its sun and sand beckons all holidaymakers ... but for me it was on to Los Angeles.

*Published by Routledge in 1967.

12

The Pacific Coast

L OS ANGELES, in the sunny state of California, I discovered, can be as cold and rainy in January and February as it is in England. But I was not there for the weather in 1961, I was in California to speak to garden clubs, which do such wonderful work in planting up byways and spreading the love of gardening in that state.

At the time of writing, there are 11,549 members of the state garden clubs in California and, in addition to their gardening, conservation, house-plant and flower-arranging programmes, they also organize a number of fund-raising events.

I was whisked around private homes to borrow vases; to markets and gardens to gather flowers and other plants; then to the venue to assess its size, and there I found the press and radio interviewers hovering. Everyone was so helpful but as everything was new and strange to me I found (as I often have done) that the pressure became nerve-racking. Although I have learned how to control my nerves a little, the tension never completely disappears, in fact the ordeal seems to get worse the higher up the ladder I climb. I do not think there is any final answer to this nervous tension. I just try to be quiet and not to expend too much energy during the preparation in order to reserve the anxiety, for it can be a power later on when released on the platform.

I really love these big events for, after giving my all – and I am never satisfied unless I have – I am happy and feel I have known the audience for a long time; and many people eventually become friends.

The southern part of California is very beautiful and I enjoyed my visits to San Diego, Palos Verdes, Pasadena, Palm Springs and the great city itself. When my talks were over I was taken to the Paul Getty Museum in Malibu which houses some of the world's most priceless art treasures. Whilst I lingered over a number of the exhibits, especially the Jan van Huijsum and Claude Monet flower paintings, it was the gardens I wanted to explore. I walked down the frescoed colonnade, looking out on to the herb garden that featured fifty different herbs, as grown by the early Romans for culinary, medicinal and religious purposes. This garden is surrounded by box hedges at the back of which are fruit trees, higher still at the back of these grow rows of the ubiquitous olive trees.

The museum building is created in the style of an ancient Roman villa, hence the style of the gardens in which, in strategic places, stand bronze casts of statues that had been recovered from the ruins of the Villa Papini, buried in the volcanic eruption of Vesuvius in AD 79. There is not much colour in the gardens, but all the trees, shrubs, flowers and herbs are similar to those varieties grown in Pompeii some 2,000 years ago. Fountains splashed in other parts of the gardens, cooling the atmosphere in this sunny spot in California.

After one of my talks in California a lady, noticing that I had used a good deal of foliage, asked if I would recommend some suitable shrubs which she could grow for flower arrangements. From the platform I quickly referred to some of my favourite evergreens such as *Elaeagnus, Choisya ternata, Viburnum tinus, Euonymus* and *Senecio greyi*. Then later in the hotel I wrote her my list, including reasons for my choice, and delivered it to her. It is as follows:

1 *Elaeagnus pungens* 'Maculata'. This golden-splashed evergreen shrub is ideal to place with the bare stems of daffodils.
2 *Lonicera nitida*. A fast-growing shrub which gives long thin stems suitable for outlines. There is a golden variety called 'Baggesen's Gold'.
3 *Choisya ternata* (Mexican orange). I love this. It has cream flower heads in spring and offers round heads of glossy green leaves, perfect for filling in and covering the 'mechanics'.
4 *Viburnum tinus* (Laurustinus). This produces round heads of duller green leaves for placing between bare stems around the centre. Gives an added bonus of pinkish white flowers.
5 *Euonymus*. Ideal for smaller arrangements. I cannot be without the variety 'Silver Queen' for all-year-round use.

6 *Cornus alba* 'Elegantissima'. Whenever you need green and white leaves for a wedding or church arrangement, this is the shrub. Let it spread in the garden and enjoy the leaves.

7 *Senecio greyi*. A low-growing silvery grey shrub which seems to withstand all weathers. Perfect for using with pinks, mauves and crimson colours.

8 *Prunus cerasifera* 'Pissardii'. I include this for its maroon colouring. It has long stems to give a background to mauve and pink flowers.

9 *Aucuba*. Commonly known as 'spotted laurel', this shrub is a cut-and-come-again one, most useful for brightening up winter arrangements.

10 *Ligustrum ovalifolium* (golden privet). I enjoy using this for large arrangements but it is not always evergreen, dropping its leaves sometimes before the new ones are out.

You can imagine my surprise a week later when, speaking higher up the coast, I read in the gardening column of the local newspaper that the garden club recommended certain evergreen shrubs for flower arrangers – then my list was reproduced. I was amused and hope many followed my advice and enjoyed the results.

Whilst driving around the highways, I was amazed to see great billboards advertising burial plots at Forest Lawn Cemetery. The billboards depicted a good-looking, grey-haired lady who stated: 'I have priced all the mortuaries and finally chose Forest Lawn.' My friend explained that everyone there buys their burial plot before they die. Evelyn Waugh writes of this phenomenon in his book *The Loved One** but, as I wanted to see for myself, we drove in, and I thought how discreet all the little memorial plaques looked dotted around the hillsides.

There are chapels or churches of all denominations and, having just finished my book *Flowers in Praise*,** about church flowers, I was interested to see how the churches were decorated. I was informed that the 'Wee Kirk' or Church of the Flowers should not be missed as flowers were planted inside in banks below the windows, the setting of which acted like a greenhouse. Alas, as a burial service was booked for that afternoon, the church was closed but, when I explained my purpose, the verger allowed me to enter. The flower planting down the sides was very colourful and looked lovely with the sun shining through the windows, and there was a huge bower of flowers standing on the chancel steps. I could not imagine how such a low, long arrangement of flowers was mechanically fixed, so I walked forward and inserted my hand among the flowers, wondering whether chicken wire, 'oasis' or moss had been used. To my horror, I discovered that I was feeling the face of the body which was about to be cremated. I withdrew quickly, thanked the verger and only relayed the story to my friends over a drink.

My time in Los Angeles was drawing to a close and I was planning my next move. I must admit that I love trains, so it was not difficult for me to decide to take the Coast Starlight that runs from Los Angeles right up the Pacific Coast to San Francisco, Portland and Seattle, with many stops in between. The coastline is dramatic with rocks and sandy beaches seen through pine trees, providing unforgettable views. I stopped off at San Francisco to give a talk to members of the Golden Gate Horticultural Society, and to visit the Botanical Gardens. Then, as the Redwood Forest was only 250 miles away, which is a short distance by car to Americans, I had to visit this great forest of majestic sequoia trees, some of which grow 340 feet high, twice the height of Nelson's Column in Trafalgar Square. The sequoias were once widespread in regions of the northern hemisphere but now only two species remain, growing in a narrow strip near the Pacific Coast. Some specimens are believed to be between three and four thousand years old. On this, my first visit, I was so moved by the experience that immediately afterwards I wrote: 'After driving along a very narrow mountainous roadway we approached the forest, and a certain hush seemed to fall over us; we did not speak. It was amazing the effect that the power of the redwoods had upon me for, as I continued on foot, alone, I started to creep as though I was in church, for almost at once I seemed to be made conscious of my own limitations.'

I entered further into their midst and stood spellbound by the sight. As you look up, the brilliant Californian sun penetrates the tips of the trees with tiny sheaves of light and, as you slowly recognize their might, you feel you want to stop and take stock of the world. I was told that each year thousands of people return to the forest to renew their spirits and adjust their sense of values. Certainly, in the shadow of these mighty redwoods, I am sure that many of our national rivalries would appear to be just family quarrels. When you see trees so invincible, so large that you can build a small house in the bole while the tree can still go on living, so vast that enough space can be carved through the trunk for a car to pass through, you have to acknowledge the force of nature.

Before leaving I took note of a poem by Jos Strauss which was inscribed in a log cabin nearby, the last verse of which reads:

> To be like these, straight, true and fine,
> To make our world, like theirs a shrine,
> Sink down, oh traveller on your knees,
> God stands before you in these trees.

Regretful to leave San Francisco, I boarded the train again going north to Portland, Oregon. Here I had engagements with the Portland Rose Society, and was able to tour several rose nurseries for which Portland is famous, the climate being similar to that in England. Today, the American Rose Society has 18,000 members, although this does not present a true picture, for one grower alone claims to sell 150 million rose trees every year. This I can well believe for some of the American Rose Nurseries are colossal. I was amazed to see tens of thousands of rose trees being kept back in cold storage awaiting shipment to some other part of the USA.

I left Portland for Seattle where there were more garden-club activities, then on to Vancouver where I took the ferry to Victoria on Vancouver Island in British Columbia. The atmosphere of the place contrasted strikingly with that of the USA for here, I felt, I was in a part of old England. The object of this stopover was to visit the famous Butchart Gardens so, after my talk to the Victoria Horticultural Society, I made my way to the curator who had promised to escort me round some parts of the gardens. I say 'some' for they cover 25 of the 130 acres of the Benvenuyo estate which began as a hobby of Mr and Mrs Robert Butchart in 1904.

The gardens should not be missed by anyone visiting this part of the world, for the skilful blending of exotic plants, trees and shrubs, mixed with native flora in a colourful series of formal gardens, which are joined by winding, restful paths, is a truly memorable sight.

*First published in 1948.
**Published by Batsford in 1977.

13

The White House

ALWAYS FASCINATED by what others do with their flowers, I had kept up a long correspondence with A R (Rusty) Young, who was the chief flower decorator at the White House in the 'sixties. As his invitation for me to visit his workrooms was always open, it was not surprising, when speaking to the British Embassy ladies in Washington in 1965, that I should let him know of my wish.

An appointment was made for 6 am as everything had to be arranged and all the rooms decorated in time for the public opening at 10 am. I presented myself at the gates and the guard took my passport. After being frisked, I was escorted to Rusty's flower rooms. There I saw huge glass-fronted refrigerators which housed a great many bowls of mixed flowers already made up. It appears that they are removed from the public rooms the evening before, placed in the cold case, then taken out again each morning until their lives are finished. Of course there are always many to be freshly made or refreshed. In the main, the bowls were composed of mixed simple flowers such as daisies, cornflowers and roses. This was the style laid down by Mrs John Kennedy (now Onassis) who felt this belonged to the period of the house, would not interfere with the many different furnishings and would act as a focal interest. In addition to the public rooms, flowers have to be arranged for all the state occasions. Table arrangements are made for official dinners given for visiting royalty, dignitaries, sheiks, presidents and others, and in each case a motif or some colour scheme is used to honour the guests. For instance, for President Giscard d'Estaing the flowers – red roses, white lilies, blue statice and cornflowers – were placed high in five-branch candelabras holding white candles, the cloths being off-white satin, printed with tiny posies of summer flowers. For President Sadat of Egypt, tall bronze prancing horses were placed in the centre of the tables, surrounded at their base with yellow and brown dried flowers with splashes of white statice,

11 This modern design from France is composed of tied arum lilies, stems beautifully curved to match the golden loops of cord and offset by the dark glycerine leaves.

12 Eremurus provide the height in this design from Versailles, with orange lilies,
bleached wood and a base of dark foliage.

13 Tall stems of ornithogalum and looped flax leaves meet at the foot of this glossy black vase, held together by leaves of variegated ivy. By the Floral Art Section, National Society of Horticulture of France.

14 A mass of summer flowers in tones of pink, blue and white displayed to great effect
in this design by the Belgian Flower Arrangement Society.

15 A collage of willow sticks forms a shapely background for the green Bells of Ireland (*Moluccella laevis*) in this free form design by IIDFA, San Remo.

16 A framework of gilded loops anchors a vertical display of purple alliums, diagonally crossed with liatris and stabilized with green ligularia leaves. IIDFA, San Remo.

17 An evocative, gentle design from the Defined Space Class, 1993 Philadelphia Flower Show, organized by the Pennsylvania Horticultural Society.

18 A massive display of yellow flowers in the conservatory at Longwood Gardens, near Philadelphia. The display is changed every month.

standing on brown, cream and flame-coloured cloths over yellow skirting. For our own Queen and Prince Philip, the theme was typical of an English garden, the flowers being lavender, Queen Anne's lace, liatris, larkspur, delphiniums, gloriosa lilies, antirrhinums, white lilies, hydrangeas, zinnias and scabious, all held in baskets wrapped round with Hawaiian ti leaves and tied with pink cords. The cloths on each table were white silk, satin striped, crossed with a pink lattice pattern holding posies of pink and pale green flowers.

On this occasion a huge white canopy lined with bushes of American Heritage and Queen Elizabeth roses covered the White House rose garden through which the distinguished guests walked to reach the house. What a glittering sight it must have been. I was told all the table decorations were later sent to residential homes and hospitals in the Washington district.

At the time of my visit, as Rusty and his assistants were busy creating the bowls of flowers, I was allowed to look through the book of full-plate colour transparencies which had been taken of the floral decorations. I would have dearly liked to possess one of these pictures but they were all firmly fixed as part of the private collection. The bowls finished, Rusty suggested I help him carry some of them into the White House and see them put into place. So, with a bowl in my hands, I walked with him down a long, red-carpeted corridor, which was flanked by portraits of famous people. Coming towards me was President Lyndon Johnson and his Lady. I tried to disappear as I felt I should not have been there but, after greeting us with a 'Good morning', the president walked on. Rusty then introduced me to Lady Bird, Mrs Johnson. We chatted and she told me that some of the flowers I had arranged the previous evening in a demonstration at the embassy had been given to her by our ambassadress, Lady Dean, and she thanked me. Later I sent her a copy of my book *Flower Arrangements in Stately Homes**, to which she replied that she hoped I had seen some of their old colonial homes.

I walked with Rusty to the white and gold waiting room with its glittering chandeliers, where he placed six arrangements on the mantleshelves, then on to the Green and the Red rooms where the walls were hung with cerise silk, bordered by gold scrolls. There was little time for me to take note of all the treasures as we passed, but I could not fail to stop and admire the huge French golden centrepiece in the state dining-room flanked by candelabras of the same period and style. I was told the flowers used were mainly white and yellow in the state dining-room, which seated 140 guests although some visiting potentates were given special treatment.

Rusty told me he had two, sometimes four, designers besides himself, constantly preparing the flowers coming from the market although, on occasions, he would also call on volunteers, but for everyday work where about twenty bowls, some larger than others, were required, he could manage with his permanent staff.

Mr (Rusty) Young has now retired and another friend has succeeded him. As I look back, along that corridor, I think how lucky the visiting public are to see such historic rooms brought to life each day with fresh flowers.

*Published by George Newnes in 1966.

PART FOUR

IN BLOOM

14

Italy

GRAND HOUSES, like the White House, have always intrigued me. My frequent visits to stay with Captain Neil McEchearn at the famous Villa Taranto on Lake Maggiore were always a delight. The gracious hospitality and the chance – in fact the never-ending opportunity – of studying the plants in this famous 100-acre garden, which he created himself, was a constant source of pleasure. We would discuss the plants for hours, he patiently explaining their origins and how he had come to possess them. Days were spent poring over his great collection of botanical books and in the seed house from where packets of unusual seeds were sent to correspondents all over the world.

The garden was a dream come true, for Neil McEchearn, a Scotsman and keen gardener, fell in love with the site as he passed one day on a train. Suffering as he did from asthma and other chest troubles, and unable to withstand his native Scottish climate, he decided to buy the site and make the creation of the garden his life's work. He was ably assisted by Henry Cocker, a Kew-trained man – all of which led to the full story being described in McEchearn's book *The Villa Taranto**.

On one of my early visits preparations were being made for the Villa Taranto's exhibit at the Triennale Exhibition in Milan in 1955, which included a horticultural show. It was suggested that I stage an exhibit of flower arrangements depicting the four seasons. I borrowed beautiful vases and props from the house and was allowed to pick flowers from the garden. Eventually I was taken to Milan where the exhibition was to be held and where I staged a modern exhibit of yellow flowers and tall twigs in a large, green-glass fruit dish to represent Spring, and a mass display in a formal bronze urn for Summer, using tall, cream, tuberose, green and cream zinnias, greeny bronze *Grevillia robusta* and ferns with bunches of brown paulownia seed sprays hanging down over the rim like brown grapes. For Autumn a large basket arrangement was made with tan-coloured dahlias, fruit, grasses and berries and, finally, for

Winter I used variegated holly and elaeagnus leafy sprays with red carnations. Everyone seemed delighted with the arrangements, and the idea initiated a great deal of interest in flower decoration among the thousands who visited the show. I was later inundated with requests for talks and demonstrations.

One lady, the Contessa Gheradesca, wrote to me in England about a year after my return insisting that I come to instruct and help a private group of ladies who were anxious to introduce the subject in Italy. I found a free week and packed my equipment, such as scissors, wire netting, vases, base boards, and dry material and with my personal luggage set off one Saturday by boat and train for Florence. Alas, when I arrived at Dover, I discovered that in my hurry I had forgotten my passport. Despite my pleas to the officials there was nothing for it but to return by train to London. As I was due to speak, on the following Monday another boat and train journey was out of the question but I was able to book a plane ticket to Milan by changing at Zürich, there being no airport at Florence. Off I set again on Sunday but disaster nearly overtook me, for instead of waiting half an hour at Zürich I mistook the announcement. I sat on the terrace and waited an hour, only to find when I reported that my plane and all my luggage had departed without me. There was no other plane out of Zürich that night so I took a late night train as far as Milan, then sat on the station and waited for a milk train to take me to Florence. I finally arrived at the hotel, where I was to speak, at about 10 am when I was also due to start, so with no change of clothing, no sleep and only a brush-up with a powder puff, I presented myself, ready to explain my plight to the countess. Without waiting for me to speak she introduced me to the ex-Queen Helen of Romania who was to be their president and, after managing a curtsy in my half-awake state, I was pushed onto the platform. I introduced myself and explained what had happened – that I had neither equipment nor flowers. Then, looking around at the eager audience who had come to be inspired, I announced with arms outstretched, 'Since you are all here, even though I cannot work, I may as well tell you about this fascinating subject.' I went on to say that never again will they walk down their gardens or even into a florist's shop without opening their eyes to the different forms and shapes and sizes of flowers and leaves, for to become an artist with living flowers all you need is to be able to place different shapes and sizes together to form a harmonized pattern. I explained, with gesticulation of hands and arms, that if they looked for tall and fine leaves or flowers for the background or outline of their arrangement, then assessed the value of the bigger or more important flowers for the centre, they need only a few more medium or lesser important items with which to fill in. As I spoke I noticed a waiter pass by, carrying a tray. I asked if I could borrow it, also some of the plants on the reception desk and some of the fruit from the dining table. With the aid of these props, plus a few large ashtrays, I made four different arrangements carrying out the principles I had explained. I spoke excitedly for two hours, gaining strength as I went along, pointing out that their awareness for colour and its uses with flowers would develop as they learned more about the subject; I added that, with experience, one becomes more design-conscious and more self-expressive, for flower arranging is like creating a picture with living flowers, and you can create to suit yourself. Some may like blue flowers, others yellow, some may like modern designs, others more formal, but whatever you do, I stressed, is right for *you* when you do it. If you change your ideas later, it doesn't matter, for art is never static.

The morning session proved to be a great success but I had no idea that there was a woman from the press in the audience. Right across the woman's page in the paper the next morning was the heading 'The British never know when they are beaten'. Then followed a report on the meeting describing how I had knocked up several arrangements with the aid of ashtrays and a waiter's tray. This newspaper report brought even more enquiries and the countess was swamped with requests for others to join the group. So great was the demand as the days progressed that I finally had to give a public demonstration, in aid of the Red Cross, in order to satisfy the demand.

Queen Helen, a keen gardener and specialist in irises, invited me to her villa on the hills at Fiesole and asked me to make suggestions as to where and how in the rooms flowers could be arranged and placed. 'I don't want you to do them,' she explained, 'for Nanny always does the flowers but, as we go round, Nanny will listen to you and, I hope, pick up some ideas.' What a gracious lady she is. We have often met when she comes to London, and she always greets me by asking: 'When are you coming to Florence again?'

I have returned to Italy many times since – what woman could not fall in love with that beautiful country, for nowhere else in the world is one made to feel more feminine than in Italy.

One recurring face in the audience almost everywhere I spoke in Italy was the charming Contessa Camilla Malvasia, who also attended all my European courses. She eventually became a leading light of flower arranging in Italy, visiting English shows, judging and teaching others. Speaking French, Italian and English with equal ability, she acted as interpreter for me on many occasions and I am happy to say our association developed into one of great friendship.

Before the flower clubs became organized in Italy I spoke and demonstrated to horticultural societies in Milan, Trieste, Siena and Rome. The city of Siena was a dream. The great open-air arena, where the annual *Palio* is held encircled by arches, the sandstone backdrop of the buildings all festooned with red geraniums, was a sight I still remember vividly.

On my way to Rome, I demonstrated to members of the Lombardy Horticultural Society, whose president in the fifties was Count Gola. The count's garden on Lake Como was a paradise. These were early days as far as flower arranging was concerned, and even for me as I travelled south, it seemed a sacrilege to be in Rome speaking on a platform when there were so many historic sights to see, paintings to admire and so much music to hear. However, a visit to the Villa d'Este, at Tivoli, the garden of a thousand fountains was a sight I could not miss, and often on reflection, when sitting quietly at home, I imagine I can hear the thunderous roar of the larger fountains and the cascades. Then, walking down the avenue of a thousand fountains, the gentler sound of the water staircase persists like light touches of music. What a masterpiece this garden is.

There are many famous gardens in Italy and many wonderful books describing them, but I would not consider Italy such a horticulturally minded nation as we are in Britain. Gardening for most people, except perhaps for vegetables, is not a mania as in England, yet they are very plant conscious, for every balcony, terrace and patio has its flowers in beautiful ceramic pots. In parts, huge plants such as cactus, agave and yucca, grow on banks and dry walls, clinging for life to any grain of available soil.

When visiting private homes at that time, I observed that the Italians seemed more conscious of the dining table and the presentation of food than we are generally, and seemed to spend more time at table than other nationalities do. Their exquisite lace and muslin tablecloths, many appliquéd with colourful flowers, and the table centres enriched with Venetian glass ornaments between which flowers were tucked, then flanked by glass candlesticks, were all a delight. Table arrangements were featured a great deal at flower shows when I first visited Italy but latterly, since the formation of the floral art and garden clubs, the trend in many parts of the country has veered towards the modern style.

This, I am sure, has been encouraged by the abundance of dramatic plant material that is available. The sculptural effects, which are made by members of floral art clubs using strelitzias, sansevieria, agave, flax, aspidistra, palm spathes, alliums, anthuriums and many other flowers and plants that are unobtainable in England, are unusually exciting. The colour blocks of carnations often recessed among large dramatic palm leaves are creations of living art. Signora Rosnella Cajello-Fazio, who is president of, and inspired teacher at, the San Remo Club, is a master of these styles, and I am always greatly refreshed when judging or admiring her members' work. She is a tireless worker for the art of flower arranging in Italy, so it was no surprise when a national organization was formed in 1986 that she should be elected its president.

There are now twenty clubs affiliated to the Italian Institute of Flower Decoration for Amateurs, (IIFDA) the outstanding artistic work of the members contributing to the floral art scene wherever it is exhibited.

*Published by *Country Life* in 1954.

15

Belgium

AS I SPENT two years post-schooldays in Belgium with the intention of learning French, I learned early in my life to love the country and its people. The atmosphere was always warm and full of expression and I look back on those carefree days as some of the happiest of my life.

So it was with great pleasure in 1950 that I accepted an invitation to join a small group of horticultural writers, led by the eminent Roy Hay, who were to visit the first great Floralies de Ghent to be staged after the war. Not that I was to be one of them: I was taken along to answer questions and man the stand that was to display their books and journals.

The flower show was the most impressive I had ever seen. In fact it still is from the point of view of spectacle. I have often been asked to explain the difference between the Ghent Floralies and the Chelsea Flower Show in London, and I think it could be summed up by stating that the Chelsea Flower Show is a garden and plantsman's show where almost any plant in the world can be seen and studied by the amateur. It is educational as well as being beautiful, whereas the Ghent Floralies, which is staged only every five years, is a huge spectacle displaying the plants that the Belgians grow professionally for export. These are laid out in a landscaped manner which is both breathtakingly beautiful and enables the visitor to cover the whole show, by keeping to the prescribed route. But there can be no turning back or retracing your steps to ask a question, for there is no one to answer it. It is, as I say, a spectacle that shows what the Belgians can grow commercially, whereas at Chelsea, which is nonetheless spectacular, the visitor is the gardener who can put questions to the experts who are there ready to answer, to explain and take orders.

The tall Comte de Kerchove, who was at that time president of this magnificent event, was originally diffident about admitting flower arranging to this prestigious show, but the persistent and patient efforts of Mlle van der Haegen and a few pioneers finally persuaded him that flower arrangers were also gardeners. In fact, as I have always maintained, flower arrangements are the end product of gardening and the arrangers by their efforts are spreading the love of flowers *and* gardening, bringing the art of arranging flowers to a very high standard.

It being just after the war, we could not take much money out of the country – the limit was £50 – so it was agreed that we take fifty copies of my first book *Fun With Flowers*, which had just been published, hoping that we might sell a few copies in order to give us a little spending money. As I was setting up the stand, two men passed by and bought a copy each. Later three more men came and bought copies. This continued and all the copies were sold before the show opened. At 21 shillings a copy, we were delighted with our riches, but I was surprised for I did not think flower arranging among women had yet reached the continent. However, I soon discovered that the books were not being bought for women, but for the growers and nurserymen who needed ideas for furthering their outlets.

Amateur flower arrangers did make a couple of forays into this great show and I remember the first effort which was organized by the early pioneers with no committee or organization. The flower arrangements were judged upstairs in a back room, then carried down to the main hall and placed as part of the decor for the show. This did not please the exhibitors, for often their displays were misplaced and even the flowers dislodged.

By 1967, the Belgian Flower Arrangement Society was firmly established with the Baronne Brigitte de Villegas as first president and Mlle van der Haegen as vice-president, and they were invited to participate. Today they hold their exhibition at the same time as the Floralies but at a separate venue, always staging a magnificent display with an international flavour.

On another occasion, after the official opening in 1975, the King of the Belgians was walking round with the president and other dignitaries when he left the party and came across to speak to me where I was standing with the other judges. After I had presented my co-judges to him he said: 'Is this your first visit to the Floralies?' I replied that it wasn't and that I had attended every one since the war. 'But,' I added, 'I might be too old for the next one.' 'Too old for what?' was his quick reply. 'Do you know that my grandmother attended this show when she was eighty-five years old?' he continued. I felt reassured by this and looked forward to attending this show for a number of years to come.

The Belgian Flower Arrangement Society today under the presidency of the Comtesse Baudoin de Broqueville, another avid gardener, has done a great deal of work in a comparatively short while. Recognizing that there should be some unification of teaching and judging, such as we had organized through the National Association of Flower Arrangement Societies (NAFAS) in Britain, they had written in 1973 asking if I would tutor a four-day course, which I was very happy to do. Representatives from France, Spain, Italy, Holland and Belgium attended, and Princess Grace came as a representative of her garden club in Monaco. Much was achieved, the enterprising and energetic Belgians repeating these seminars at regular intervals, adding other tutors, until today we all feel we speak the same language of flower arranging. The society also organizes competitions and exhibitions that are sometimes staged in private houses, at other times in castles. I recall an occasion once when there was to be an exhibition of flower arrangements in the Château de Laarne. The visitors were suitably dressed for an evening function and, as we drove up in a long line of cars, I was taken aback by the sight of this floodlit moated castle. It appeared like a picture from a fairytale book. I asked if I could get out of the car and walk. I wanted to absorb the atmosphere and wondered when and for what reason such a magnificent edifice could have been built. I am always afraid that I might never again be given such an opportunity. I long for more time, yet there seems always to be such a rush. As we walked from room to room admiring the furniture and the splendid displays of flowers, I wondered what the early owners would have thought of such an intrusion. Yet today, sharing is commonplace and it is the intruders who help to keep these historic places alive.

I had no idea there were so many magnificent châteaux in Belgium. The members of the society need never be fearful of running out of venues for these displays, which convey their love of flowers, their free artistic style always shining through. They love the mass bouquet and, as the flower arrangement movement in Belgium is more of an upper-

middle-class expression, this flowing style suits the elegant backgrounds of many of their homes.

To mark the entry of Britain into the Common Market in 1973, the
Belgian authorities had organized Europalia, a month-long tribute to
the British arts. British ballet was staged, British music played, British
painting displayed, a choice of films was shown, antiques exhibited
and, to my great surprise, English flower arrangements were to be part
of the programme. I was very pleased to be invited to take part in this
event, and chose as my theme 'Flower Arrangements in English Churches'. The stage was all in black, which I decorated with white flowers,
the first part of the programme being a showing of slides of English
church flowers, the second part being a demonstration using all-white
flowers with church music playing in the background. In order to avoid
a solemn atmosphere as the large audience entered, I chose the cantata
'The flowers are blessings' from Benjamin Britten's *Rejoice in the Lord*.
As far as I know, it was the first time a demonstration had been conducted to music.

Since that time, the Belgian Flower Arrangement Society has gone
from strength to strength. It has 26 delegations, with 2,300 members
who are active in organizing, teaching and judging courses in all areas.
They work closely with France, Italy, Holland, Monaco and other
European countries, exchanging ideas, and have awakened the love
and artistic use of flowers in the home. The society's exhibits are some
of the major attractions at important events in the city of Ghent, and
this led to them becoming the host country for the Second World
Flower Arrangement Show in 1987. Opened by Her Majesty Queen
Fabiola, the show proved to be a tremendous artistic success.

16

The Magic of Monaco

ONE MORNING, early in 1965, my secretary came hurriedly into my office waving a telegram. As she placed it on my desk she hovered nearby, wondering who might have sent it. It was from Princess Grace of Monaco inviting me to go to Monte Carlo to discuss the formation of a garden club and flower show.

I was so excited I could not pack my bags quickly enough to fly out to Nice. The sun was shining and the palm trees were swaying in the balmy breeze as I walked across the airport tarmac. I was met and driven up that winding road, which overlooks the harbour, to the palace high up on the rock. Ushered by a footman into an elegant sitting room I noticed several ladies already present including Madame Arpad Plesch, Madame Paul Gallico, Madame Paul Demange, and Madame Louise de Vilmorin. We stood up, I then curtsied as Princess Grace entered the room with those smooth rhythmic movements that were so typical of her, and surely were the result of early training. I was surprised at her gentle and soft American accent and the way in which she grasped and analysed every suggestion put forward. I cannot think why I was particularly surprised; perhaps it was because I had imagined that she would listen and then hand over to a committee, but no for, as with everything she undertook, she was very thorough. The garden club of Monaco was formed then with Princess Grace as president and soon after, the first brave effort of a flower show, with flower arrangement competitions, took place.

As judges we were individually given the complicated European judges' sheets that indicated the system whereby points had to be allocated in a number of columns headed: Colour, Design, Scale, Rhythm, Shape, Plant Material, Originality, etc. I could foresee that it would take even a competent mathematician hours to arrive at a decision, the result not always being what we expected. The unfortunate secretary, Monsieur Giovannini, who was also the supervisor of the gardens in the principality, was working frantically in order to arrive at some decision for the press. It appeared that this system of judging would have to be changed.

After the opening of the show by Princess Grace, who was accompanied by the Sovereign Prince, Rainier III, and their family, we were invited to the palace to tour the gardens, which were in full bloom, it being the month of May. What a magnificent view there is from these remarkable gardens high up on the rock. The mountains loom majestically on one side, whilst from another angle you can see the precipitous drop down to the sea. From another opening through the trees you can look right out over the harbour full of yachts and sailing boats bobbing up and down. The roses were prolific, blooming much earlier there than they do in England. As we walked around, a lady-in-waiting asked me not to leave when the others did, and directed me to the Princess's office. I sat and waited. Princess Grace appeared with notebook and pencil and said: 'Now, tell me, have I gone wrong anywhere?' 'Nowhere,' I said. 'I thought it was a great success.' 'But tell me how I can improve it,' she asked. We then discussed staging, niches, good schedules and, of course, a more simplified method of judging.

She made masses of notes, and due to her enthusiasm and guidance, the next show was a tremendous improvement. Painted backdrops were hung high from the walls of the vast Halle de Centenaire, niches were provided in which each exhibit could be seen separately and the revised method of judging went like newly oiled wheels. But perfectionist as she was, Princess Grace wondered how the show could be made more international. I suggested writing to various countries overseas to obtain some of their indigenous plant material and for it to be put on display. It was early days and, although the material arrived, there was little experience among the members of the Monaco Garden Club to display it to advantage, so I offered to make large non-competitive designs. Beautiful rhododendrons, so difficult to grow in the principality, which arrived from the Royal Horticultural Society's gardens in England, I arranged in a huge stone urn. Prince Rainier loaned me an African carved head that I surrounded with proteas sent from the famous Kirstenbosch Gardens in South Africa.

Madame Arpad Plesch loaned me two exquisite Chinese cloisonné vases for the Singapore orchids. Not wishing to stand these vases side by side, I announced that I would very much like a tin or a box on which to stand one of the vases above the other. Such a tin was eventually delivered to me, and I draped it with a Chinese shawl on which the two vases stood, one above the other, holding a swerving design of orchids. Some years later I learned that when I asked for the round tin on which to stand one of the vases, a messenger was dispatched to the Hotel de Paris, where they emptied a large tin of caviar, because Miss Clements wanted the tin for the Princess's show. However, these large overseas exhibits created great interest, and every year since there have been some improvements. The International Concours de Bouquet is now an annual event much looked forward to by the populace and overseas visitors alike.

Princess Grace was very knowledgeable on the finer points of floral art, having judged at the Ghent Floralies, at San Remo and in the USA. She attended all the European judges' courses in order to keep up to date. Once at an instructional course, she was listening so intently during the morning that I did not think she would return for the afternoon working session. But she did, and made a remarkably clever arrangement of strelitzias with blue irises, oranges and yellow peppers. She was so pleased that she asked if I would accompany her back to the palace to decide where to put it, 'so that my husband will notice it', she added. It was placed on a small table right opposite the lift to her sitting room. 'There he cannot miss it,' she said. I heard later it was highly praised.

She was a truly sincere garden and flower lover; her pressed-flower pictures were beautiful and original, and were snapped up at every exhibition where they were shown.

I have been invited back every year since that first visit in 1965 to judge, teach or conduct a course. Once, after dinner at the palace, we adjourned across the courtyard to what previously had been a coach house, but was now effectively appointed as a cinema, there to watch a film. We all stood around chatting, chocolates and liqueurs being offered; then, at some sign being given, a liveried footman appeared carrying an embroidered foot-stool with carved legs and placed it in front of the Princess. We sat down and I turned to her and said, 'How lovely, but what is the stool all about?' She replied, 'Our doctor said that every woman over forty should put her feet up whenever she can, so my husband bought me this for my fortieth birthday, and I love it.'

On another occasion when we were walking round the palace gardens, I noticed a bed of the lovely pale pink Grace of Monaco rose. I laughingly said: 'I've got you in my garden, but I see you haven't got me in yours.' 'Oh, something must be done about that,' she said. However, on my return home I arranged with Mattocks of Oxford, the rose growers, to send out a dozen Lady Seton roses which were planted later with Fleur Cowles, one of Princess Grace's close friends – Madame Meilland – and other rose-loving friends.

At every visit, whether on flower-show work or not, the magic of that principality never fails to touch me. The cleanliness of the streets – not a stray piece of paper to be seen – the courtesy of the inhabitants, the beautiful gardens, the fountains, the baroque buildings so reminiscent of the Belle Epoque (now alas, some of them overshadowed by modern skyscrapers), are all there to be seen, if you have time enough to stand and stare. All of this magic, as well as art exhibitions, and concerts given by the Monte Carlo Philharmonic Orchestra, also visits to the Jardin Exotique (the finest of its kind in the world), are added to the flower-show weekend.

One of the most interesting classes of this flower show is that devised by Princess Grace herself, for 'Men Only'. Her charm would pull in over the years such personalities as Paul Gallico, Marc Bohan, David Niven, Michael York, Karl Lagerfeld, and many other visiting celebrities. Another of her innovations was to invite famous people of artistic talent, such as couturiers, musicians, artists, interior decorators and writers, to judge separately from the official panel of judges. This artistic panel based their judgement on such standards as the best colour scheme, the best design, best use of plants, most original exhibit and best sense of humour.

Prince Rainier himself is no mean flower arranger and I remember a design he made of mauve flowers and grey foliage with asparagus, it being a Vegetable and Flower class. A piece of twisted iron, like a clamp, held up the asparagus. He won second prize. I learned later that his hobby is iron sculpture.

At the 1983 show we were all deeply saddened by the absence of Princess Grace, but she lived closely in all our hearts. Before leaving that year, we, the judges, placed flowers on her tomb in the cathedral. No one could have foreseen the tragic accident that took place but she had sown seeds to bloom again and again. Not for nothing was she christened Grace.

Her flower-arrangement show, which has become international in its appeal attracting entries from all over the world, still flourishes with Princess Caroline as president of the club and show. She also is knowledgeable about plants and flowers, her artistic touch is noticeable in the staging of the show and wording of the schedule and, watching her as she stands with an assured presence, handing out the prizes, I feel her mother would have been proud of her.

Today, on land reclaimed from the sea, situated near the stadium and heliport, a new town, Fontvielle, has arisen among fourteen acres of landscaped gardens. With its artistically designed flower gardens, lakes and olive grove on different levels, its waterfalls, rose arbours and stupendous sculptures set against a backdrop of the mountains, it is an aesthetic oasis on this sunny coast. Standing in the paved, circular courtyard of the Place de Campanile, where the Church of St Nicholas stands, it is hard to believe that, only a few years ago, waves swept over this land. It is this special area, near where the flower show is now held, that the Princess Grace Memorial Rose Garden has been established. In addition to the garden's 5,000 flourishing rose bushes, there is also a bronze statue of Princess Grace by the Dutch sculptor, Kees Verkade.

17

France

THE CHOICE of Paris for the Third World Show of Flower Arranging in 1990 under the presidency of Marie-Hélène Leduc was a great triumph for France, for the French seemed to be a little late in the rush for everyone to take up flower arranging as an artistic expression. Yet there was a definite interest, I recall, as early as 1960 when Madame Christianne Schmidt had organized an exhibition under the wing of the National Society of Horticulture in Versailles.

I remember judging and demonstrating at this show in 1960, which must have been the forerunner of the floral-art section formed by the National Society of Horticulture of France. The members of this section still support the annual Versailles show and, in recent years, under the auspices of the city of Paris, they hold their own prestigious annual show and demonstration in this beautiful city. Under the presidency of several talented women, their advancement has been dramatic, the imagination and artistic presentation of their exhibits is acclaimed even among the artistic milieu of the discriminating Parisians.

Usually, after judging in Versailles, we were taken on a pleasure trip, perhaps to an art gallery or museum, a theatre, or to some famous garden. I recall my visit to Malmaison with pleasure: the Empress Josephine spent her last days here and here she established her famous rose garden. If roses are your particular interest you should not fail to visit the superb rosarium at Le Haye. There are many beautiful gardens and châteaux not far from Paris, the most famous being Vaux-le-Vicomte. I went alone one day by train and was amazed at the extent of the formal gardens laid out by the renowned Le Nôtre. It was a long walk from the station. Arriving on foot I went first to the gardens and lakes where I felt a man, who could have been a guide, watching me. As I went into the château, I noticed the same man following me. Every time I stopped, he stopped, and each time I made a note I could feel him almost peering over my shoulder to see what I had written. I could not shake him off. Finally I asked if he wanted something of me. He replied that he did not, but he wondered what I was doing for he could not understand why a woman alone and without a car, would walk all that way to see a garden. I smiled to myself thinking he did not know garden lovers. In his book, *The Fringes of Power,** Sir John Colville writes that Elizabeth II on her first visit to Paris after becoming queen, remarked that Vaux-le-Vicomte was the most beautiful garden she had ever seen. It is certainly one of the best I know and should be visited by all who are near Paris.

On another occasion the judges and I were taken to the opening of Princess Grace's exhibition of pressed-flower pictures in Paris. It was a glamorous evening with Her Serene Highness, standing almost like a statue on a slightly raised dais, receiving guests. She greeted us all lovingly – I thought at the time I had never seen her looking more beautiful – and we took photographs of her. As I walked around, I noticed that nearly all her pictures were already sold. I wish I had been able to buy one myself; it would now be worth a fortune.

The flower clubs in France are now very active, following the energetic guidance of Marie-Hélène Leduc and her committee. In December every year all the flower clubs hold a floral show entitled *Noël Enchanté* on the same day throughout the country, which is scintillating in effect and full of ideas. The proceeds are given to organizations working for the benefit of sick and handicapped children.

The enthusiasm expressed by the committee every time I meet its members is being passed on with great success and flower-club membership continues to increase throughout France. Today there are some 60 flower clubs and schools affiliated to the National Society of Horticulture which, among other benefits, helps to train demonstrators and increase publicity. Three times a year examinations are held on the skills of flower arranging, the knowledge of plants and historic flower paintings.

This same enthusiasm was evident at the Third World Show held at Bagatelle in the Bois de Boulogne in Paris 1990 when, in addition to their National Exhibition, which was so varied and unusual I could hardly bear to leave it, 362 other exhibitors from 21 countries also attended to compete with the world's best.

The French have an inborn artistic quality that allows them to place forms, shapes and colours together, whether they be of fruit, flowers or leaves, in a veritable still-life picture. It seems to me that we in Britain approach flower arranging as from the garden, whereas the French see a colourful design in forms. Not for them the rule of 'one and a half times the height of the vase'. Once the basics have been mastered, the French say 'Let's make a picture'. The whole city entered into the spirit of the 1990 World Show with the mayor of Paris, Monsieur Jacques Chirac and Madame Chirac giving a party in the Hôtel de Ville that included many government ministers. It was not only the large exhibits that attracted the thousands of visitors, but the small touches on the tables, the walls and high up on the mirrors, denoted also that we were in artistic France.

*Published by Hodder and Stoughton in 1985.

PART FIVE

IN FULL FLOWER

18
South Africa

WHAT DREAMS of this vast country I had conjured up ever since I had read *King Solomon's Mines* as a child. For years I had visualized the vast spaces, the wild animals, the exotic plants, the jacaranda and flame trees. Who were the Zulus? I would ask myself in my ignorance, and the historic rise of that great city of Johannesburg had always intrigued me, and still does. Yet somehow, although constantly travelling in various parts of the world, South Africa never seemed to come my way.

I should explain that most of my travels have been brought about by the invitation of different organizations who invite me to judge, demonstrate, teach or speak. So you can imagine my delight when, in 1977, I received an invitation from Mrs Lola Hudson Bennett, the president at that time of the Durban District Horticultural Society, to judge and officially open the great Flower Show in the Durban City Hall. I had understood, through correspondence, that a high standard of floral art existed among the members, but now I was about to see for myself.

My first sight of the Jan Smuts airport in Johannesburg, with its vast sculpture by Danie de Jager, immediately made my spirits rise. It was new, it was different. Here I had to change planes for a short flight to Durban, and when I saw the smiling face of Mrs Lois Armitage of the Natal panel of judges, I felt assured of a happy visit. It was. In fact from that moment onwards I felt both at home, yet in a different world.

I was driven all along that rugged coastline of the Indian Ocean to the ranch-style house of Mr and Mrs Ladlau at Umhlali, and what a sight confronted me. The climate being sub-tropical, almost everything exotic, plus annuals, perennials and roses, seemed to be growing together in the garden. It was easy to pick out anthuriums, strelitzias, arums, clivias, heliconias, and leucospermum in one part of the garden

whilst, in another more shady area, I noticed delphiniums, antirrhinums, roses and poppies and a host of various ferns. Any flower decorator would be tempted to jump with delight at such a choice of
colour and variety. Bougainvillea tumbled over the roof of the guest
house, and in the more wild parts of the garden, great cones, as well as
bark, pieces of wood and fallen branches, could be gathered.

For a flower arranger it was a paradise. Inside the house Rosemary
Ladlau, a talented flower arranger and former chairman of the panel of
judges, had created some superb flower displays that emphasized even
more the type of exhibit I might see at the show. Press and radio
interviews followed and next day came the show. The sun was shining, everyone seemed uplifted and I was most impressed by the pat-
terned bedding gardens which surrounded the City Hall and where,
although we arrived early to judge, crowds had already started to
form.

The competitive flower arrangements on display were dramatic and
much larger than we in England had been accustomed to seeing. Huge
pieces of driftwood five feet high would hold one spray of cymbidium
orchids, the design being finished low down with exotic fruits and
bromeliads. Large branches were fixed into modern-style pottery containers, some of which held red anthuriums and bunches of green
bananas and cocoa palms. I saw also large fans of black sea fern, studded with diamanté, sprouting from tall twisted, burnt black ivy root,
the centre of the design being emphasized with red amaryllis. It was
all very exciting and pointed the way to the future. In the Pedestal
class, great bunches of bougainvillea swerved down at the sides, the
centres being filled with azaleas, anthuriums and roses. I would have
preferred not to see the anthuriums, for they seemed incompatible
with spring flowering shrubs but then, as I have said, in the gardens
they were all blooming together.

Not everything at the show was huge and dramatic: some of the
most dainty flower arrangements I have seen were exhibited in the
Light as a Feather class, where fine tendrils were associated with tiny
flowers in exquisite glass, and some tall glass candlesticks held bleached tendrils, flowing downwards with tiny skeletonized leaves and
white daisies. Exhibitors came from Zimbabwe, Cape Province, the

Transvaal, and the Orange Free State, as well as from Europe and the USA. Everyone was happy to express their own ideas with flowers. It was February, the sun shone daily, it was warm and I felt almost light-hearted among so many flower friends. I could not accept all the kind invitations that came my way, as reluctantly I had to move on but I knew I would have to return one day.

I travelled on to Cape Town where another engagement awaited me. Here the climate was hotter than in Natal, but activity within the flower clubs was much in evidence. At that time Sybella Skelpe, so active in the floral-art world, told me that there were nine flower clubs in Cape Town itself, affiliated to the Association of Cape Flower Clubs. Prior to the formation of this association, the Cape Adjudicators' Union had helped with and judged floral art. The clubs' art work is of a high standard and continually changing, for their eyes are always open to new ideas.

There is a Judges' Union in each of the four provinces of the Republic of South Africa and Namibia, each union belonging to the South African Floral Adjudicators' Union which strives to maintain uniformity through the whole of the vast republic.

On my way to the Cape I passed what seemed to be a sea of blue agapanthus. Here I must digress for, writing of agapanthus, I am reminded of a true story that was told to me in Australia of a lady who lived in the outback, miles from any neighbours. She had few friends or social life, but often travellers stopped by to ask the way and, periodically, tinkers called displaying their wares.

She was a keen gardener, and one day when searching through a catalogue she came across the name of a flower she did not know. She sent for the bulbs and planted them with great hopes. Some time afterwards, she noticed the shoots appearing through the red soil. Excitedly, she watered them and was impatient to see what they were like when in flower. Afraid that any calling tinkers might wheel their barrows over them, or even walk over them, she placed a notice on her garden gate which read 'Be Careful of the Agapanthus'.* Unfortunately, from that day onwards, in her unwanted loneliness, she never had a social or tinkers' call again.

The only previous time I had seen agapanthus en masse was in the home of Mrs Blandy in Madeira. She had placed about thirty cut stems in a large brass-rimmed wine cooler standing in the hall. They made a great impact on me, especially as I have to check my purse at home before buying even five!

Whilst in the Cape I was able to pay a visit to the world-famous Kirstenbosch Gardens. Set among the lower slopes of the majestic Table Mountain, they presented a superb sight. Proteas of all varieties were growing profusely over the slopes, whilst in the lower parts of the gardens there were all kinds of colourful ericas (heathers), George lilies, nerines, crinums, clivias, flame lilies, and so many other beautiful flowers, which we in England cherish in greenhouses but here flourish in abundance in the open.

I have written of mountains on my Canadian Rockies journey earlier, where all was white with snow and ice, but here this great range of mountains, excelled by the flat-topped Table Mountain enveloped in mist, was covered with brightly coloured wild flowers. An impressive sight indeed.

General Smuts, the great world statesman, philosopher and a former prime minister of South Africa, often wrote that as he strode near the mountains he could respond to the individual appeal of the flowers and was constantly absorbed in their wonder. Truly, the south-western part of the Cape peninsula is one of the floral kingdoms of the world: some 24,000 floral varieties can be found there. How lucky I have been to be able to visit these wonderful sights through my work.

Later I went on to Stellenbosch, where I had the good fortune to have Major Phillip Erskine as my guide around the many private gardens that exist in this area. He, a former president of the South Africa Antique Lovers' Association, and his wife Fiona, have restored their historic Dutch-styled home and furnished it with authentic Dutch colonial furniture. I contemplated the gardens, the outdoor living and the sunshine, and could not help thinking what a beautiful country South Africa is. 'If only I could stay here permanently,' I happened to voice to a group of ladies. Then one of them looked up and said: 'Before you make your decision, you had better be careful.' Careful of what I wondered. I had seen only beauty, kind people, smiling faces, beautiful flowers, lovely gardens. I had seen black people with happy faces sitting on the lawn of Mr Ladlau's garden waiting for their pay, and I had seen black people carrying heavy loads of wood and flowers into the show for the ladies. Why must I be careful? I wondered. I knew so little of politics, and even less of apartheid, but I began to wonder if flowers might play some small role in helping people understand and accept each other. But, of course, this was only a dream.

I have, however, come to realize that there is no greater common denominator in the world than flowers. They are universally recognized and loved. They have a common language and are not manufactured by one country exclusively, nor are they any one person's particular invention or right. They are nature's gift to everyone. The more the flower clubs spread their work among all peoples the better it will be, as that common language spreads its universal message. Were the original flower people right when they offered a flower to everyone with the message of love not war? Princess Grace once said that you have to open your hand to hold a flower and, although it may seem a simple thought, we might take an example from the flowers, whose silent lips do not decry or envy each other. Perhaps it is all too simple, but many simple ideas have produced great things. We, as individuals, can only set examples; given the thousands upon thousands of happy flower arrangers there are in the world, these could be a mighty force for global harmony.

But to continue with my tour of South Africa – on leaving Cape Town I flew to Johannesburg where I was to speak at a luncheon organized by Joy Fleming and Georgie Shillcock at their country club. Johannesburg struck me forcibly. I sensed its vigour and could not at first believe that this great modern city, with its marble-seated post office and towering skyscrapers, was just a quagmire a mere hundred years ago. It might still have been but for the discovery of gold.

The avenues of purple jacaranda, the luxurious houses, the swimming pools and gardens all drew me but, as a short-time visitor, I had no time to venture further than the city and its residential suburbs.

In Pretoria, I was able to chat to Marie Pretorius, the president of the flower club, who told me that the vast province of the Transvaal was divided into eleven areas all of which are more or less active in flower arranging, according to their proximity to a town. In Pretoria alone, the capital of the Transvaal, there were ten flourishing flower clubs, but all the areas combined to exhibit in their important show, Flora, which takes place every two years. In between times they stage smaller shows in aid of charities and, at that time, were planning their exhibits for the Jacaranda Festival in conjunction with the Parks Department. This is a very special show. Being so much further north, the plant material differs from that in the Cape, for in the Cape there is winter rainfall, whereas in the Transvaal the rainfall is in summer. The most prolific flower growing in the Transvaal was, I noticed, the Barberton daisy or gerbera, which is native in this Province and which we in England love to use when it is imported.

I also visited Elsa de Jager, the flower arranger and wife of Danie de Jager, the famous sculptor. This meeting was a great eye-opener, revealing how far one can go in this supposedly domestic floral art. For here Elsa picks up shells, bones, sea fern, coral, broken branches and dry pieces of plants from the arid surroundings, then welds them together in her studio, creating some of the most dramatic flower sculptures you could ever dream of. I add the word 'flower', for a flower or plant added here and there go to complete the imaginative works that constantly gain the top prizes wherever they are exhibited.

As we sat over tea by the lakeside near her modern-style house, colourful exotic birds strutted out from the bushes here and there, and I heard of her feeding a baby elephant which they had rescued. As she drove me over the dry dusty track back to Johannesburg, where I was to board my plane for my return home to England, she constantly made notes of interesting pieces of wood or bone that she would pick up on her return, and I am sure a saw and a drill would help her to produce another masterpiece. Elsa is unique and I was happy to have made this visit.

As promised, I returned to South Africa to judge at the next Exotica in 1980, which was opened by Mrs Katherine Hedley of the USA National Federation of Garden Clubs. More friends were made and more exciting exhibits were seen. Who says that flower arranging is not an art attracting people from all over the world? Flowers can be expressed in the hands of a sensitive arranger as eloquently as a musician conveys his emotions through an instrument. Certainly this time the exhibits were even more expressive in colour and interpretation and better staged. It always seems a pity that these exquisite works cannot last longer on display, for flowers are ephemeral and after some days they have to be dismantled.

After the pressure and excitement of the show, the organizers decided that the judges should be taken on safari. We drove for a number of hours in four cars and, after checking in at the entrance of the Mkuzi Game Reserve, where we were allocated several huts, we unloaded in preparation for the evening barbecue. Darkness seemed to fall quickly and although we could hear the call of some of the animals, we decided to go to bed to get some sleep before making an early start the following day.

In the morning we separated, driving in different cars to various areas to view the animals. At night we all sat around by the light of the barbecue and swapped stories of what we had seen, with some of us exaggerating a little. It was eerie at night as the fire went down and the rustle among the bushes seemed to come nearer. The men of the party played tricks on me and my co-judge, Marian Aronson, by scratching at our hut door and making growling noises. We sat up warily at first, then after realizing the trick we tucked up and slept soundly until the next morning.

I was surprised at the height of the giraffes nibbling greenery from the tops of trees and quite often we saw groups of the gentle-looking impalas. We also watched zebras and wart hogs wandering through the bush. Later we watched some sable antelope, and two of our party saw leopards; it seems they stay up in the trees during the day, only to prowl at night. We all enjoyed the 5 am rises and the barbecues in the darkness over which stories were exchanged. We were sorry to leave and, in fact, nearly did not at that time, for we were brought to a halt by a huge giraffe which darted out from the bush, bumping into the first car then managing to jump over it. The driver said it might have been difficult explaining to the insurance brokers in the city that his car had been hit by a giraffe. However, the damage was light, so we continued. On the exit road I saw a notice announcing the name of a waterhole we had not visited and, as I was in the last car, I asked if we might look in just for a few minutes. We turned in and, after parking the car, we walked along a long, narrow sandy pathway with a high wattle fence either side until we reached the watch house. Notices for Silence were everywhere, so we crept up the steps and took our seats looking out from slits in the walls of the hut.

I looked down to a shallow pool with muddy surrounds, beyond which there seemed to be a large bare patch of ground backed with trees. At each side of this barren patch were more trees and shrubs, and my mind went immediately to the thought that it looked like a stage set. No one, I thought, with the greatest of imagination could have conceived a setting more appropriate for a ballet. All was silent, nothing but the set was visible, our binoculars, though quite heavy, were held as though they were feathers in case their weight was sensed by the animals, our breath was held, we did not speak, always conscious of the Silence notice, and then – yes – three antelope, one behind the other with a studied grace, looked around suspiciously, sipped some water and then walked off the other side. Was this the overture? I asked myself. We continued to watch in silence. Then, among the trees at the left, we perceived a number of zebras. They came, looked around, then went, finally returning, when all seemed clear, to partake of the water. They stood, stared, and looked around again and then went away. Was this *their* act? Before I could nudge my companions I espied a little dancing group. It was a mother, father and three little wart hogs who, with their twenty twinkling legs, pirouetted towards the water like a corps de ballet. They sipped the water, the father, leaving his leader position to gather up and push the little straggler at the back to the edge of the pool. They stayed together, but instead of going off the opposite side, they turned round and made their exit along the path by which they entered. My eyes could not be everywhere and, whilst I was watching the wart hogs, my companions were nudging me to look elsewhere. We did not speak, we hardly dared breathe. Apart from my experience in the redwoods of California, never have I felt so close to the Creator. Then, from what seemed like back stage, a dark mass appeared. What was it? We couldn't ask each other. It came forward. It stood, it looked around, raised its head, came further forward to centre stage, kept turning and looking around, but did not come front stage to the water's edge. Then, with a final bow, it turned and

19 Lichen covered branches add height to the clustered white peonies in this Canadian design, balanced on the left with looped flax leaves and held in a brown leather container.

20 This modern design from the Florida Garden Club features orange lilies, purple liatris and clipped palmetto leaves dramatically posed with the two cylindrical containers.

21 Another unusual container, holding strelitzias and a palm leaf for height, balanced with shaped palm leaves in this elegant American design.

22 An abstract design from the Cape, South Africa, composed of tall palm spathes, strelitzias and king proteas. Note the 3-D effect.

23 Sea fern, circled sansevieria leaves and thorn branches make this delicate
design from the Transvaal, South Africa.

24 'Spirit of the Forest' is the title of this design from New Zealand. Large puka leaves, loops of lawyer vine and tree fern descend from the top of a clay pipe.

25 'Haere Mai', a Maori welcome. The Maori totem pole is decorated with ferns and flax leaves, with folded pseudopamix leaves and loops of lawyer vine at the base.

26 Julia Clements outside Buckingham Palace after receiving the Order of the
British Empire from the Queen, February 1989.

walked off. It was a rhinoceros. The scene continued, each separate breed of animal appearing at different times. They did not come together and fight for the water, they silently took their turn. Is this the way it was, I thought, each one taking its turn and knowing its place? There seemed to be no competition. Where were the predators we are told about in the wild? Perhaps they were not in this reserve, but the whole play, as we watched it in silence, was a lesson in behaviour. I looked at my watch and, instead of the few minutes I had requested, we had been there two hours. We left in silence, to speak would have broken the spell. In fact we were halfway back to Durban before we could bring ourselves to voice our views of that waterhole, an experience which I shall never forget.

On my return home to England, I frequently thought of the behaviour of the animals at that waterhole. They all seemed to walk quietly to the water's edge, then almost in silence lap up a little refreshment and leave, allowing the others to take their turn. Where was all the violence between animals that we see on the films and television, the tearing at each others' throats, the fighting and chasing? I wrote to David Attenborough asking why it was that they all took turns, with no one fighting for the front position. His reply was that animals only fight each other when their territory is threatened or when hungry. Was this, I wondered, the reason for revolutions, or is this also too simple an answer?

*Agapanthus is a tall umbelliferous flower belonging to the lily family. Its bare stem rises from a bed of strap-like leaves and, in Britain, it is mainly grown in tubs on the patio or in greenhouses.

19

Mexico, Costa Rica and Guatemala

I HAVE OFTEN found myself in some strange places on my journeys. On one occasion in Kansas, as there was no venue available for an evening performance, I agreed to appear in a basement disco in the afternoon. All went well until someone behind the scenes mistakenly pressed an automatic background music switch half way through my talk. Utter confusion reigned, for I was caught up in flashing coloured lights and beating drums. It was some while before the offending switch was turned off and, of course, the whole thread of my talk was lost. I started again.

Not only strange venues but also odd sleeping places come to mind. I've had the pleasure of sleeping in the homes of millionaires and the experience of sharing the same bed with my hostess in a small town. But none of the experiences seem as unusual as the one which led me to stay in a sleazy hotel in Mexico City. I had no official engagement there but, on my way from Los Angeles to Costa Rica, in February 1980, I had a few days to spare, and the opportunity of diverting my journey to Mexico City seemed too good to miss. I phoned a lady with whom I had been in correspondence, who then begged me to conduct a workshop for her club members after my arrival. I was excited as the plane descended and I listened to the Mexican airline hostess who, over the intercom, gave a potted history of Mexico, its conquerors, its language, currency and political background. She also gave me the name of an hotel – 'not very expensive'. 'I will phone them,' she said. After passing through customs with the aid of four different porters, each one passing me on to a friend and each one demanding payment, I asked for a taxi. The driver accepted me, then waited until he had filled his taxi with three more travellers. After depositing the other passengers, I was driven into what seemed like the suburbs to a poor-looking hotel. My spirits dropped. Yes, they

130

were expecting me, but no porter was available, so I dragged my heavy luggage up three flights of linoleum-covered stairs to what seemed like a large attic room, for the small window was high above my head. The light switch was hanging loose from the wall socket, so I was afraid to try to turn on the light for fear of being electrocuted. It was nearly dark, but I noticed another wire leading to what I thought would be the bedside lamp, but no, this lamp rested on a shelf some distance away. So, after getting into bed, I had to get out again to turn off the light. The room had no lock on the door and I was scared. Nevertheless I slept well.

The next morning I contacted my garden-club friend, who invited me to join the club's visit to a monastery garden where there was to be a talk on ancient biblical plants. I walked silently round the garden trying to identify the plants. We all walked quietly, some taking notes, until the atmosphere was heightened by loudspeakers hidden among the trees issuing sepulchral music that echoed across the grounds. It was quite moving. Later that day one of the members took me on a tour of the city. I was stunned by the sight of the cathedral set in a vast square which seemed greater to my eyes than that of St Peter's Square in Rome. The wide avenues lined with trees, each roundabout full of flowers, was another unexpected sight. The huge fountain in the courtyard of the famous Museum of Anthropology caused me to stand in amazement, for the water seemed to travel up the inside of the structure, then burst out over the top and tumble down over protrusions here and there. The effect was wonderful.

The vigour of the brush strokes and the almost violent colourings that never seemed to clash in the paintings in the art galleries struck me forcibly. I was attracted to all of the exhibits, especially the painting of the white galloping horses with glaring red eyes and flared nostrils on a black background. It was almost frightening and I wondered where it would eventually find a home. I vowed that whenever I had the time to satisfy my yearning to paint, it would be to Mexico that I would go to study.

The next day had been planned for teaching. When my friends called for me, they were horrified by the place where I was staying but it was too late to change, especially as I hoped to visit Cuernavaca. The ladies I was to teach arrived, bringing mauve, pink and blue flowers as they wished to practise what they termed the English style. These flowers seemed so delicate and pallid in comparison to the vivid orange and purple colourings I had seen in the paintings.

I made my visit to Cuernavaca, where Mexican history begins and ends with the imposing Aztec pyramids. I did not have time to visit the pyramids, but friends arranged for me to visit four private gardens which were hidden behind high walls, all covered with tumbling flowers, including flame-coloured bignonias, cerise bougainvillea, and climbing ipomoeas (morning glory). I was so moved by all I saw that, before returning to Mexico City, I bought a huge volume on the history of the Aztecs meaning to study it on my return home. I still have not done so. It was then back to the hotel to prepare for an early departure to Costa Rica the next morning. I asked for a 5 am call and a taxi to take me to the airport, and was assured all would be done. I awoke at 4 am, an hour before my alarm call, as one often does when expecting a call, but no call came, so eventually I dragged my heavy cases down the three flights of stairs and caught sight of the night porter sound asleep on a bench. I shook him and asked about the taxi. 'No problem,' was his half-awake reply but, as there were only two flights out of Mexico a week, I was becoming anxious. After ten minutes a battered car pulled up, the driver, with a long drooping moustache, looked like someone out of a macho film. I jumped in the car and said, 'Airport, quick.' He drove at a frightening speed down narrow side streets and screeched round corners on two wheels – he could have been taking me anywhere. In the half-light between dark and sunrise, I saw his hairy thick arms and began to think 'if only my friends could see me now'. . . . We reached the airport and he lifted out my luggage, saying with a sense of achievement, 'Plenty time, si?' He then bowed to me and smiled, showing a mass of white teeth. Looking at him with some relief, and with a new awareness for I had thought that he might have been a Mexican bandit, I saw him then as a gallant gentleman.

An invitation to be a guest at the International Conference in February 1980, hosted by the garden club of Costa Rica, had conjured up my wildest dreams. Exotic flowers, beautiful gardens, sun and sea – then I had to stop, for where *was* Costa Rica? I had only a vague idea but, after studying a world map, I cabled my affirmative answer.

But first let me explain the reason for this visit. It appears that every year the garden clubs of the five nations in Central America (Panama, Nicaragua, Costa Rica, Guatemala and Honduras) combine to support the host country that stages a week-long conference on flowers, indoor plants, conservation, judging techniques and, of course, a flower show and a number of social events. In addition, an overseas visitor is invited to judge, speak and demonstrate, as guest of honour. I was to be that person on this occasion.

Arriving at San José airport in Costa Rica, I was met by the president of the festival, Señora Carmen Montealegro, a most elegant lady dressed in a fine flimsy pink and green gown, and wearing very high-heeled shoes. She looked very feminine and I felt that some gallant man, or even I, should help her get to her car with my heavy bag. Her looks deceived me, for she picked up my large suitcase as though it were a few bunches of flowers, and threw it into the back of her estate car and off we drove. We continued in what seemed like wild country-side for some distance, passing en route rows of corrugated iron-roofed shacks which I presumed were the suburbs of the city, or per-haps villages, with women and children sitting on the pavements.

As the country evened out she pointed to the left and said: 'That's my husband's coffee farm.' Turning right, we drove down a long drive into a dell which unfolded a view of an attractive ranch-style house surrounded by trees. As we entered the open door into the hall I heard splashing water, then saw that it was falling from an outlet high up in the centre of a double-sided staircase into a pool below which was surrounded by ferns and other water plants. It was all so refresh-ing, green plants seemed to be everywhere. As I was led to my room I wondered whether I should first satisfy my curiosity by exploring the house and garden or whether I should study the programme of events which my hostess had handed to me in the car. I chose the latter. When I could see there were so many parties and events planned for every hour of the day, I changed my mind and decided I had better try to visit the theatre where I was to speak and demonstrate the day following the opening of the show, in order to assess its size.

Unlike a straightforward talk or lecture, where the lecturer stands composed behind a podium on which his notes rest, a flower-arranging demonstrator must first know the size of the platform and the hall, and must also know the audience capacity in order to plan the size of the work to be demonstrated. Then there are the types of vase that will be required and which must be borrowed and, of course, where and how to acquire the flowers. None of this can be done in advance of arriving in a strange place, or rehearsed. This and much more was rushing through my mind, but the town was seven miles away and I had to be patient. Drinks were served. *Mañana*, I could feel, was in the air. The garden, set on several levels, was beautiful and as I sat there, viewing it from the large open patio, I was mentally reserving certain plants that I might use on the day.

Only those who have experienced this worldwide demonstrating can understand how the tension starts to build up immediately on arrival. You are searching for answers to all your problems but visitors arrive and, over drinks, wishing to be social, they start talking about the good time to which they are looking forward, and about how marvellous last year's demonstration was in Panama. You sit trying to tune in quietly and furtively ask what type of flower arrangement they like. You get no lead, so you then try to find out about the theatre, and it is explained with great pride that their national theatre is the most beautiful building in the whole of Costa Rica. 'How big is it?' I ask. 'Well it is all gold with painted ceilings, elegant staircases with chandeliers, in fact, it is just like the Paris Opera House' – then, after a pause – 'but a little smaller.' I was thankful for the afterthought but, oh dear, I now began to reassess all that I had mentally planned. I then paused, accepting that I could do nothing about it at the moment – it was all to be another day.

Next day came the judging of the show. There were so many judges being briefed that at first I thought there must be more judges than there could be exhibitors but with so many competitors from so many different countries, a number of judges from each country had to be included, as well as invited judges, such as myself, and those from California, Florida, and other American states. All went smoothly and, after the decisions were made, which included awards for creativity and colour, there was a rush to prepare for the official opening by the First Lady of Costa Rica, Señora Estella de Carazo.

The opening was in the evening, and this was followed by a dinner, held in the open air under trees festooned with tiny coloured lights. There were tables each side of a long carpeted gangway at the top of which was the head table at which the president of Costa Rica sat. At the right of the top table was a rumba band. On each of our tables there were glasses plus bottles of rum, gin and whisky with buckets of ice and mineral water — no need to be waited on, you helped yourself. In the centre of each table was a huge model flamingo, the framework and legs being made of heavy copper wire, the body being covered with closely packed pink flowers. I started to look in my handbag for a pencil to make note of all that was happening but, before I found it, the rumba band started with its pulsating beat and almost everyone got up, swayed their shoulders and danced with anyone who was nearby, whether it was man or woman.

Finally, with a roll of the drums, everyone sat down and then, one by one, each country's garden club president was led in with a uniformed escort carrying her country's flag. With her national anthem playing, she walked down the long red carpet to take her place at the president's table. The night was warm, the band intoxicating, and the dancing continued long into the night, but my own thoughts kept going back to the size of that theatre.

The following morning I spent gathering flowers and borrowing vases. Matters were beginning to take shape but there were no strelitzias or anthuriums in the market, flowers that I expected to find in such a climate. However, a lady promised to bring some strelitzias to me for the demonstration. I was then taken to the magnificent theatre, the ladies promising to return to help after their cocktail party. No one came but can you blame them for it was fête time? I was happy to work alone all through the day. I decorated one side of the stage with white and pink flowers, placing palm leaves and orange, red exotic flowers on the other. In the wings, I prepared my vases and placed beside each one the appropriate flowers as I would need them in demonstration. These were all laid out in their colour schemes on a long trestle table and covered with a damp cloth to keep them fresh. I felt quite satisfied as I was driven back to the house where I changed for the evening performance to which the president of Costa Rica had been invited.

Can you imagine the horror I experienced, on my return ten minutes before the curtain was due to rise, to find that that my materials had been moved all over the place because, it was explained, the stagehands wanted the table. They all had to be retrieved and sorted out again. The strelitzias arrived but they were garden grown and were twisted – never mind, I used them at the sides. The theatre was filling up, the plush curtains were down. Then, as I was still searching for my flowers and vases, the house rose and clapped at the president's arrival and the playing of the national anthem. The interpreter arrived, rehearsing the introduction. The tension mounted. 'We're late,' someone shouted. 'I'm not ready,' I answered. 'But the president is seated,' he said, and yes, the curtain was rising. I was on. The interpreter, Mrs Adelita d'Odio, was excellent, picking up on every innuendo of my talk. The flowers behaved perfectly, going just where I wanted them to. After two hours I felt so good I could have continued for another two hours.

The president of Costa Rica, Señor de Carazo, gave a champagne party after the performance and in conversation he told me that he did not have an army in Costa Rica, only police. Knowing the proximity of El Salvador, a trouble spot at the time, I said: 'Without an army are you not afraid of being attacked?' 'Not at all,' he replied, 'why should I be afraid of attack, I am not going to attack anyone.' Then he added: 'After listening to your talk about flowers not fighting for supremacy despite their various sizes and colours, I think you and I should get together, we might make a better world.' What a lovely thought. And so it was over except for the clearing up but everyone was happy, myself in particular, for the audience was one of the best I have ever had.

The next morning the programme consisted of a visit to a famous private garden which I was sorry to miss, but I had to go back to the theatre to collect and return the vases and other items I had borrowed to their respective owners. I felt relaxed and pleased that all had gone well and returned to my hostess who was offering a large barbecue and cold buffet to all the exhibitors and officials of the show. It was warm and sunny and all the ladies were in light colourful dresses, and wearing high-heeled shoes. Some sat by the pool-side, others on garden seats dotted around the hillside, whilst others, in order to avoid the sun, sat on the covered patio among the huge containers of medinilla — that gorgeous plant with hanging racemes of pink flowers.

Various languages vied with the clatter of plates and cutlery, and then a strolling band arrived. The players serenaded each group as they wandered around the garden, passionately singing to anyone whose eyes they caught, their own colourful costumes competing with those of the ladies. Everyone was enjoying themselves. Their exuberance was catching to the point that when I reminded the afternoon lecturer that she should soon be moving, she replied: 'Oh I'm not going, I'm having too much fun here, why don't you do it?' This seemed to be the mood — something else took the lecture's place and no one minded — we were in Latin America.

I was fascinated by the women in this part of the world. They walked provocatively, they changed their dresses three or four times a day, at least during the conference. Sometimes their hair was down, to be tossed as they turned around, at other times it was swished up, sometimes even to one side, and always there were flashing eyes over the shoulder, as if searching for approval. Had I been too serious, I began to ask myself.

I then reflected that flowers had certainly brought me a long way and, as I looked up at the flower-covered hills surrounding the house I noticed how tall the palms and lantana bushes were and, making a mental note of flowers that I knew I should never be able to grow, I considered that I was lucky to have had this opportunity of seeing them.

One more day of lunches and meetings and then the farewell dinner. Members from each country were asked to wear their traditional costume and they were also warned that during the evening they would be asked to act, sing, play or create a charade which typified some aspect of their country. My hostess wore a bright crimson silk skirt with layers and layers of white lace petticoats, and a typical Costa Rican embroidered white muslin off-the-shoulder blouse with a frilled top studded with coloured sequins. On her feet she wore high-heeled red satin shoes. She looked lovely. The evening was billed for 8 pm, but this meant nothing (we did not eat until 1 am). Bottles of all kinds of drinks were on every table.

Soon after our arrival the throbbing of the rumba band started and everyone got up and danced with everyone else. I followed suit swishing my skirt like the others and was surprised at the steps that emerged from my feet. Between each session of dancing to the main rumba band, the various countries presented their acts and I sat back and wondered what would happen if we invited clubs in England to put on such shows. Was it the sun, or the drink, or the rumba band that released all their inhibitions? Perhaps it was a little of each but the air of gaiety was infectious.

I had to leave the next morning at 5 am to get to Guatemala, the only plane to go out that week, leaving at 6 am. Just after dinner, therefore, it being nearly 3 am, I was very anxious to get away. However, as president, my hostess could not leave before the rest of the company, but she promised that her husband would call me in the morning to take me to the airport. I eventually got a lift back to the house and went to bed at 3 am. Up at 5 am, I was worried about getting to the airport for there was not a sound coming from my hostess's room. I walked up and down outside their bedroom door, I coughed, I dropped my suitcase heavily against their door, but no movement or sound emerged. In desperation, I finally burst into their room and shook the poor husband, who jumped out of bed. I then kissed my sleepy hostess goodbye and we set off. The sun was beginning to rise as we drove along in silence. It was no time for him to point out various aspects of the countryside. On lifting my bags out of the car, he told me that he and his wife had reached home only at 4.30 am. I wonder if he has ever forgiven me. . . .

Sitting in the crowded airport waiting for the number of my flight to be called, I was alone and at last able to reflect on all that had happened. No more questions to answer I thought, no more smiling until I reached Guatemala. Though tired, I was happy and relaxed. I then noticed a lady carrying some dried flowers coming towards me.

She smiled and said: 'It was a good show wasn't it?' I nodded in agreement but wondered how or if she knew me. She then continued: 'I've been watching you – you must be Julia Clements, for you are to be my house guest in Guatemala.' It was dear Hilda Asturius, and it was all to start again.

Guatemala, home of the Mayas, with its chain of volcanoes forming the highlands on the Pacific side, was to be my resting place for the next five days and I took to it at once. Naturally in so short a time I can only claim surface impressions but these should not be discounted. I asked myself why it is that in some countries one immediately feels a warmth, yet in others one is not affected at all. Here it was as though a hand stretched out to touch me. Was I feeling more aware because of my relaxed state? I sensed immediately a feeling of kindness, of caring; there was a noticeable showing of dignity and I knew I would enjoy my stay.

On the day of my arrival I was driven to the lakes, where it appears most people of a certain class have a weekend house. The roads were dusty and the verges dry and strewn with litter. Further out into the country there was little green to be seen anywhere. It appears it rains there for six months, then is dry for six months, and my visit coincided with the end of the dry season. Although they were all longing for rain, it did not bother me for it was the month of February and my thoughts went back to England where it would be cloudy, cold and raining. Nearing the lakes, the hilly countryside became much more green with charming gardens surrounding the weekend houses. Seated in a comfortable deck chair with the gentle sound of lapping water just reaching my ears, I soon fell asleep, for I had been up and travelling since 5 am. Then suddenly I was awakened by the ground moving and all the tea things being shaken off the table. 'What was that?' I cried out. 'Oh that's nothing', my friends replied, 'only a tremor.' Remembering the 1976 earthquake in Guatemala when 25,000 people were killed, I cried: 'What do you mean, nothing?' They then explained that they would always get an official warning if there were a real earthquake, so I asked why they hadn't had a warning in 1976. They explained that it was all the old buildings and churches that had come down, under which people were buried, but now everything was built in a different manner.

After a delicious meal, we drove back to the city and I went to bed early in preparation for the next day's work.

I say work, but it was going to be a delight, for the members of the garden club requested a four-day teaching programme. They explained that they were tired of competitive work and wanted some other aim, something to satisfy them. So, after having passed the great cathedral in the Parliament Square which was still in ruins from the earthquake, funds being in short supply for the complete rebuilding, I suggested we spent our training days in learning church decorations. A further suggestion was that they should hold a non-competitive flower festival in the church. This would allow each member, whether she was advanced or only a beginner, to make some kind of floral offering. And so the days of teaching started.

The flowers were prolific in the Guatemala markets, much more so than in Costa Rica, it being much further north. The market was full of every imaginable variety, with many exotics besides. There were many interesting plants in the gardens and I was able to pick branches of mauve solanum.

All were brought back to the home of one of the members, at the side of which was a large four-car garage open at the sides, where we were to work. We practised making large pedestal groups, swags, then garlands and, on another day, altar flowers and window-sill arrangements; everyone becoming more and more proficient in the making of different shapes to suit particular settings. I explained the importance of publicity and the allotment of certain positions in the church for the members of varying degrees of flower-arranging experience and ability, and everyone was satisfied that each was playing a part without the supposed attraction of winning a prize.

The days passed all too quickly for, in between lessons, I was taken to some of the Mayan culture reserves where I am sure Bill Gibb and Yves St Laurent would go crazy at seeing the outstanding patterns and colours of the hand-woven fabrics.

Finally, a small exhibition of the members' work was held which uncovered a great deal of latent talent. I was loath to leave these kindly people. A buffet party was given for me on my last evening in yet another lovely house. Amid the hubbub of fifty chattering voices, I wandered out among the ferns and climbing flowers in the illuminated walled garden and kept asking myself: 'Is this really me in this walled garden in a flimsy dress in February in Guatemala?'

During the flight home the next day I wondered if they would ever carry out the ideas suggested in the lessons. Two months after my return I received some coloured photographs of the flower festival held in one of their churches.

20
India

A GARLAND of flowers was gently placed round my neck as a sea of smiling faces greeted me on arrival in Calcutta in 1986. I was there at the invitation of the Pushpa Bitan Friendly Society to give demonstration teaching in English flower arranging to their members.

Like South Africa, India had always intrigued me. I had read a number of books on the continent, I had collected many travel brochures and had also retained all the articles on India that ever appeared in the *National Geographical Magazine*, yet when questioning myself I was never sure what it was that attracted me. Whether it was the people, their religion, their music, their culture, their whole way of living or a touch of mysticism, I did not know, but here I now was and I was determined to find out.

The morning after my arrival I was taken to the market to buy flowers: my dream of India had not prepared me for the shock of the street scenes in that great city of nine million souls. Masses of poverty-stricken bodies squatted on the sidewalks, sheltering under pieces of canvas or cardboard, living, sleeping and dying in holes in the walls. Everyone who could afford it went by car no matter how short a distance with the hope, I presumed, of shutting out the dreadful sights. For nothing, I was told, can be done individually and in the end you get used to the poverty. Many of the buildings were decaying, or without paint, yet to the seasoned traveller who could turn a blind eye to the street scenes, Calcutta had much to offer in the way of arts, the races and the museums left by the British. But flowers were on my mind. In the market I found them tightly packed behind glass panels in small shops, which were crowded in among shops selling shoes, jewellery and food. I was so bewildered as I had hardly recovered from my long flight that, after watching a number of men squatting on the ground making floral decorations or garlands, and placing flowers into baskets in a flat, fan-shape design, I left the purchasing of flowers to my Friendly Society friends. How these ladies managed to step over the mess and the rubbish, plus the bodies, in their beautiful saris, amazed me. But they did. Most of them possess about sixty saris, so can change and send them to the laundry or dry cleaners at will.

We returned to the house where I was staying, where we recut the stems and placed all the flowers in deep water. As I looked out from the terrace on to the green lawn and noticed all the shrubs and ferns, I felt I was in a different world. I pinpointed a number of leaves and ferns that I wanted to use the next morning then, after lunch, I was taken on a tour of four different gardens. These were full of lush and exotic foliage such as crotons, philadendrons and palms, with short-stemmed annual flowers low in the front of the borders. At each house there was generous hospitality: I was served with tea, cakes and other Indian sweetmeats by gentle ladies in colourful saris. I loved the small decorative hand wash basins placed in a corner of the dining rooms. It was explained to me that the body's vital energies are cut off if a knife or other implement is used whereas, by picking up food with their fingers, the spiritual energies are passed back into the system.

Early next morning I watched the erecting of a huge canopy in my hostess's garden under which the ladies would sit whilst I demonstrated on a raised mock platform. A hundred ladies attended each day and everything went well; a sense of serenity seemed to pervade. In the evenings I gave several illustrated talks to other societies on flowers in English churches, stately homes and other events, such as shows, the curiosity about Britain being considerable. Although it was perfectly understood that events like Britain's church flower festivals could not be staged in India's Hindu temples, the women enjoyed seeing the masses of flowers.

Flowers are strongly featured in daily life in India. Garlands are offered on arrival and departure and at special events, such as when I was a guest speaker at a flower exhibition. These garlands are made with flower heads of oleanders, hibiscus, marigolds, or other short flowers threaded onto string. But it was the floor flower-petal arrangements that attracted me. As most of the floors of the better-class homes are of stone or marble, the flowers are laid on the floor in a pattern, sometimes representing a festival or other event, sometimes just to spell out a welcome to a guest. Many hotels depict their logo in a floor flower-petal pattern only to have it swept away and replaced the next day. I was a guest at a flower show staged by the members of the Pushpa Bitan Friendly Society who organized all kinds of festivals that happen throughout the year, and anyone who knows India will agree that there are a great many.

There was great excitement at this event. No one had told me television and radio officials would be present. Perhaps it was an example of their tendency towards understatement. I felt under-dressed in comparison with all the lovely saris.

Driving back I was drawn by the purple bougainvillea and flame-coloured bignonias which climb up many of the white-washed walls of the smarter homes, and always, it seemed, the large lawns were green. I asked the reason for this and was told that the dew each morning was always very heavy, like a light rain.

In addition to daily lessons I was able to squeeze in a visit to the Agricultural and Horticultural Society's annual show that was held in Calcutta each February. I was impressed, not only by the variety of the plants on display but also by their quality. There was also a competition and large display areas of flower arrangements. The society, founded in 1820, was very proud of the fact that during all those past years they have worked towards promoting and improving horticulture in India.

A concert given by the world-famous Ravi Shankar was an added delight, for his sitar playing had appealed to me, as it has done to thousands of others. After playing continuously for two and a half hours he stood up, picked up his sitar and walked off the stage into the wings. My emotions were high and I was ready to stand up to applaud but he did not return. Was this an expression of non-claiming I wondered, or a portrayal of the submission of ego as practised by the Hindus? Either way, it taught me a lesson.

After a week, as I left for Delhi, my generous hosts assured me their flower work would continue with greater zeal. I knew very little of Indian history but I understood that Delhi had the most continuous and longest history of any city in India. In the last three thousand years it has seen the rise and fall of great empires; having been ruled in turn by the Hindus, the Muslims, the Moguls and the British, plus short invasions by others.

Alas, I could not linger in this beautiful city of New Delhi, but I made a tour of the Government House and the magnificent garden designed by Sir Edwin Lutyens which surrounds it.

A quick visit to the Lodi gardens also proved well worth while. The Lodi family (1451–1526) seemed to have created this great park as 'a home for memorials'. At one time, there were fifty great octagonal domes, and numerous smaller ones all set among the flowers, lawns, ponds and trees. The majestic larger domes still dominate the garden as does the dome of glass with its blue enamelled tiles and painted floral designs. Excellent views of the city can be obtained from the top of the double Persian dome but, alas, I did not have the time to climb to the top of the roof. The flowers and shrubs seemed similar to those we grow in England, the beds being laid out in Victorian fashion with annuals, and I saw deutzias and other flowering shrubs, and heard tales of the masses of colourful rhododendrons.

The stories reminded me of the tales my late husband used to relate. He, Sir Alexander Seton, was born in Naini Tai in the hills outside Delhi, where he spent the first nine years of his life, his father being Colonel Sir Bruce Seton, Indian Medical Corps and surgeon to the Viceroy. I used to hear of the azaleas and the flowers that grew in the hills, thinking, in my ignorance at the time, that he was exaggerating. He was not. But now I had to move on to Agra, as does every visitor to Delhi.

My story is not meant to be a travelogue. Today almost everyone has their travel stories to tell but my own travels are always connected with flowers. Yet in Agra I had no such engagement. Almost everyone has seen pictures or has read or heard stories of the Taj Mahal, the great marble edifice, which was commissioned by Emperor Shah Jahan as a memorial to his wife who died after the birth of their fourteenth child. The fine marble was brought from the quarries near Jodhpur and the jewels and precious stones that were used for inlay decorations came from all parts of the world. The mausoleum took twenty-two years to build using the skills and work of twenty thousand men. The result is magical. I saw it during the daytime, then went back at twilight and sat on a stone bench in the silence. The air was still and, as I gazed in the fading light on this magnificent monument, for a time my mind seemed empty; I was very moved and just stared. I asked myself why I was there, how did I get there, what did it mean for me? I was awakened from my dreams by one of the keepers, reminding me it was after closing time and, as I walked out past the now closed little shops in the avenue leading to the main doors, I looked back in an effort not to lose the atmosphere. Outside the gates the trinket and souvenir sellers were moving off. I reached my hotel still, it seemed, in a dream and, not wishing to eat, I went to bed. I could well understand the remark made by our present Prince of Wales when he visited the Taj Mahal recently. He said: 'He must have loved her very much.'

On to Jaipur. Indian airports can be quite frightening for the crowds were enormous, the bustle and noise greater than I had known elsewhere. I was told to join a general queue for security checks only to find after half an hour that I was taken out of the queue as my flight was being called elsewhere (so, no check). Why they could not have a separate queue for each flight I do not know. Everyone offered to help but I did not know who was official or who was not, for few seemed to be in uniform. Yet somehow it all ended well and I was on my way to Jaipur, the pink city. Most readers of about my age will recall with pleasure that glamorous couple the Maharajah and Maharanee of Jaipur, who graced the London scene for many years before the Second World War. They were always one more reason for my wishing to visit India. After 1947 and Independence, the Maharanee wrote *A Princess Remembers*,* which is the most romantic yet saddest book I have ever read, and so it was to the Rambagh Palace, where the Maharanee used to live (now an hotel) that I made my way.

Jaipur is one of India's loveliest cities. Avoiding the poverty-stricken street scenes, there is an aristocratic elegance about it with its wide streets, imposing buildings, all in coral pink brick, and the now empty palaces and forts. Anyone interested in studying the history of flower arranging should certainly make their way to Jaipur, for here painted on the walls of the Amber Palace and the forts are the most exquisite examples of flowers in vases of either embossed or inlaid marble of various colours, some even of mirrors, all created during the Mogul period (1526–1857). The vases (there are dozens of examples) appeared to have a Persian influence, some containing flowers alone, while other paintings showed flowers with fruit in a lower bowl. I saw no reference to animals or people in these wall paintings, only flowers. Writing of vases, I could not help staring in amazement before the great solid silver vase, five feet in diameter which stands outside the present maharajah's residence. The former emperor took this vase, filled with holy water from the River Ganges, on all his journeys. It was brought with him when he came to England to attend Queen Victoria's Jubilee celebrations.

I watched camel carts (Jaipur being near the desert) trotting lightly down the wide streets, threading their way among the crowds, which were dressed more colourfully than in other cities. Orange and red saris vied with the bright pinks and yellow, the female populace wearing much gold and many trinkets. I spotted the oleander-garland sellers, who sit outside the temples. The ladies wear these garlands into the temples to be blessed. With one eye on those prostrated on the ground outside the temple, I watched groups of children dancing to the haunting sounds made by a wooden pipe. The cows and the roaming dogs, the myriads of bicycles, all mixed in with the crowds seemed like one colourful amorphous heap.

Back to the Rambagh Palace Hotel where the surrounding gardens are magnificent. Bowls of tuberoses scented the interior whilst outside there were banks of rhododendrons, and several gardeners constantly preparing and planting the beds. Then on the marble floor of the terrace I watched one of the men create a star-shaped, flower-petal design. The colours were purple, yellow, green and pink. When I asked if the wind would blow it away, the reply was, 'There will be no wind.'

On to Udapoor, where I was to give lessons, and what a wonderful sight the Lake Palace Hotel is, set in an island in an azure blue lake. Its dazzling white marble reflected in the water makes it a 'must' to visit. Built in 1740 as a summer palace for the maharajah and his lady friends, here the wall paintings were different from those in the earlier Mogul Palace, and depicted dancing girls and hunting scenes. The silk furnishings and crystal in the rooms, which surround the lotus-filled pools and terraces, are typical of the royal taste in decoration. Now an hotel, the terraces are the favourite place for tourists' cocktail gatherings.

My plane was hours late, so the lessons were cancelled, but I was amply compensated by my visit to this island fantasy. Then it was another plane on to cosmopolitan Bombay.

When I arrived at the airport, there was no one to meet me. It was chaotically crowded and I was surrounded by men offering to help me. Eventually I found a phone but my hosts were out. I tried ringing hotels but they were all full. By midnight I accepted an offer of help from a man who led me across a railway line, down a small cul-de-sac and up three steps where another man said he was expecting me.

I was taken upstairs to a narrow corridor leading off which were a number of small cubicles. There was no light in my room and no lock on the door, above which a glass panel allowed in a little dim light. I stood still for a while, wondering whether it was worthwhile to undress, when the door was pushed slightly open and a voice asked, 'Can I come in?' I told him he could not and asked him what he wanted. He replied that he thought that it was I who wanted him. I dismissed the idea that he might be there to offer a light bulb, pushed a chair against the door and my luggage against the chair and went to bed.

The next morning there was no coffee or restaurant available but I was able to telephone my hosts who apologized saying that they had waited for my plane at 10 am not realizing that my arrival time was 10 pm. I was relieved to see their car arrive and as I stepped in, I asked the chauffeur the name of the hotel, adding that it had been awful. He replied, 'That's not an hotel, that's a brothel.' Oh dear. . . .

After this somewhat inauspicious beginning I found Bombay to be a striking city. I had heard of its squalor but I did not see it. The two-and-a-half-mile marine drive, with the water almost lapping the promenade was a real surprise, and the main hotels fronted by well kept gardens were grand and opulent. The flower displays in the modern Oberoi Towers Hotel were notable, created mainly with amaryllis and anthuriums, not one or two, but dozens of them. I later learned that they were arranged by Mrs Mullinck, who works ten to eleven hours a day there, not as a 'profession' she told me, but because she loved it. She was delighted to see me, having read my books, and she took me to her workshop where bunches of amaryllis stood in buckets of water beside other exotic flowers. She told me she spent about £1,000 every week on flowers and, where previously the amaryllis was imported from Holland, a local man now grew them specially for her.

I had lunch in the nearby famous Taj Hotel, where everyone meets everyone else, and where flowers in copper urns abounded. Then a visit to the Kapoor Theatre, just outside Bombay. This open-stage theatre was set among trees and, seating three hundred, was planned by the late Jennifer Kapoor, the sister of Felicity Kendall. After saying goodbye, Shashi Kapoor, Jennifer's husband, known by all Indians as the Laurence Olivier of India for his acting and directing of films and plays, called out to me: 'Remember me to Geoffrey and wish his book well for me.'**

My hosts in Bombay were the flower-loving and generous friends of my hosts in Calcutta who promised, on my leaving, that their doors would always be open to me. It was all a wonderful mind-stretching experience. I loved the respect that everyone showed to the elderly, I loved their graciousness and their uncrital acceptance of each other. I was impressed by the closeness within the family and when I asked some ladies what, in their opinion, attracted an Indian man to a woman, thinking it might be their beauty, their hair, their ankles or their dress, after a short silence, they replied that it was dignity. And that impression has stayed with me.

---

*Published by Weidenfeld and Nicolson in 1976.
**_The Shakespeare Wallahs_ by Geoffrey Kendall, published by Sidgwick and Jackson in 1986.

21

India Revisited

I NEVER DREAMED when I left India that I would return two years later. But it so happened that I was invited to inaugurate the twentieth anniversary Flower Arrangement Exhibition by the Kusumika School of Floral Art in Calcutta. This allowed me to stop off in Delhi on my way out giving me a longer stay than before, and enabling me to visit the many historical sites I had previously missed. Contrasting with the bustling crowds one sees in Calcutta, here in Delhi it was less crowded, the avenues were wide and spacious, lined with flowering trees, the roundabouts everywhere planted with colourful flowers. My eyes were always on the flowers but, on one occasion at a buffet luncheon, when I presumed I was off duty, I was asked to make a flower arrangement. With relief I replied that I could not as I had no flowers or vase or holders. 'But *we* have them,' was the reply, and there, hidden behind a table, were some flowers, a bowl and a pinholder. I could not refuse.

I toured the alleys and side streets of the old city. Everything happened on the streets, sometimes in the open, sometimes under shacks. There were stalls selling all manner of items, including pots and pans, vegetables, jewellery, shoes and sandals, bicycle repairs, and freshly cooked food. There were also dressmakers and furniture-makers, working adjacent to one another. The jostling crowds, the smells and the atmosphere were intoxicating, and the kaleidoscope of colour was riotous. I wondered how all these people could earn enough to live on. Yet in contrast, not far away was the city of New Delhi which was an astounding sight.

New Delhi is the most successful twentieth-century planned city yet built. Designed by Sir Edwin Lutyens to administer an empire, it is now government headquarters for a single country of about 700 million people who speak over 1,600 dialects.

The historic Red Fort cannot be missed; it dominates the city and is visited by thousands every year, but I was in search of more wall paintings of flowers and inlaid marble examples of flowers in vases, so after passing through the great Lahore Gate, I made my way to the Diwan-i-am. What exquisite vases were here portrayed. The flowers in them appeared to resemble tulips. Where they had come from, who grew them and where are the gardens now? These carvings, like those in Jaipur, are of the Mogul period (1526–1857). The Moguls (Afghan warriors and men of industry and wealth), lacked the culture of the Persians but often married the more cultured Persian women, hence the Persian influence in the style of the vases. The Fort itself is massive; you can drive round the outside for thirty minutes before reaching the main gates and everything inside is remarkable. The marble palaces facing the ornamental courtyards, the Painted Palace, the Hall of Private Audience with its costly silver ceiling studded with thousands of tiny pieces of mirror, all need time to be studied. The silver ceiling and the inlaid floral designs in these Halls, with their gilded arches, and polished marble, have witnessed the rise and fall of the Moguls, but the spirit of this architectural wonder is captured in the inscriptions engraved above the arches:

> If on earth be an Eden of bliss,
> It is this, it is this, none but this.

There was too much to see in one visit, and at one time I had to sit quietly in the peaceful garden near the Pearl Mosque and close my eyes whilst listening to the trickling of the fountain. 'This is India' was all I could muse to myself, the India I used to dream about when, as a young girl sitting in a dark room with the door closed, I played on the piano, 'Pale hands I loved beside the Shalimar'.

A visit to the Mahatma Gandhi memorial was equally moving. A broad footpath, flanked by quiet gardens bordered with ageratums and candytuft, leads to this *Samadhi* (a shrine of black marble on the banks of the River Jumna, where Gandhi was cremated). On the shrine are inscribed the last words he uttered on being assassinated: '*He Ram*' (Hail God). There were flower-petal designs on the black marble and a pad of closely grouped marigolds, which is renewed and placed there daily.

Another day. Another visit. This time to Indira Gandhi's home which is also a shrine open to the public. As I walked in I saw a panoramic view of her life in photographs. Photographs of her as a child, at university, with her father Pandit Nehru, of her own Presidency, and of the visits of world leaders including Ronald Reagan and Margaret Thatcher; they are all there. Much more moving is the tour of the outside of the house where the walls have been removed and replaced by plate glass, so allowing visitors to peer in and note the contents of the rooms, just as they were on the day she walked out of the house with her own bodyguard who shot her.

I moved on through the garden and shrubbery to the spot where she was shot (now covered by glass), opposite which there is a marble dais suitably inscribed and guarded by two armed soldiers. I stood in silence trying to understand why it had to happen. Other visitors were approaching so I dropped a single flower on the marble and reluctantly moved on. There is so much more to Delhi than monuments and history. The public gardens are peaceful, the climate is wonderful from October to March, the hotels, with their block-type flower decorations, are superb, much more modern than I have seen in many other cities and, when I viewed a number of visitors relaxing on their sunbeds beside the hotel pools, I decided that the next time I came to Delhi it would be for a holiday.

But now, on to Calcutta where I was to inaugurate the Floral Art Exhibition in the Fine Art Gallery. The exhibits were well staged and showed great artistry, some depicting the festivals of India with floor patterns of coloured rice and seeds highlighted by flowers, others illustrating different aspects of history, such as a spinning wheel around which were grouped white flowers and white wool; another showed a bridge, at each end of which was placed a different religious flower symbol with the title 'Bridging the Gap'. No admission fee was charged, Mrs Uma Basu, the founder of the school and organizer of the exhibition, stating she would rather people were introduced to the art and be made more conscious of nature than be charged admission and perhaps stay away. Coloured slide shows were enjoyed, and more lessons were given; sometimes in elegant old houses where gracious living was still practised, with white uniformed servants wearing red turbans serving tea on the terraces. The lawns were green, the flowers in the tubs were fresh and colourful, so unlike my mental picture of an Indian garden, but the contrasts are great in this vast country. During my visit everyone seemed to be talking flowers.

February, I was told, was a popular month for weddings, so I was delighted to be invited to a ceremony to be held in a large garden. Part of the garden was covered by a raised floor. At one end a *pandal* – a form of canopy – was erected over the marriage dais on which stood two gilded, elaborate throne-like seats. On a backdrop to the marriage dais leaves appeared to be stitched, whilst leaves and flower garlands were twined around all the poles. In between the poles were hanging decorations of larkspur and roses held in wet sand in bamboo boat-shaped containers, all carefully made by Kavita Poddar, a leading member of the Pushpa Bitan Society.

I did not discover when the ceremony started or finished for a priest was reading passages continuously from certain poems relating to fertility and good fortune. The couple sat motionless and all the while the guests were strolling about the garden eating and drinking and chatting. Groups came up to the dais and threw some rice, others blessed fruit, sweetmeats, coconuts and offered them, then wandered off again. All the while I was trying to understand the sequence of events. The ladies wore their most elaborate saris and jewellery, some children played whilst others danced during the ceremony. I left the wedding for a while to attend the prizegiving at the Agricultural and Horticultural Society's annual show and, when I returned, the wedding was still in progress, the bridegroom leading his bride round the sacred fire four times, the fire being the witness of their vows.

The next day I attended a pre-wedding party where a huge chandelier-type of arrangement of twisted palm leaves hung from the centre of the canopy in the garden. Here four thousand pot plants of coleus, marigolds, celosia and zinnias had been banked up around the trees and borders. Apparently nurserymen deliver and arrange the pots, so that they appear as a huge mound of growing flowers, they then remove them when the wedding parties are over.

In addition to all the flowers, one great honour was still to come my way. I was to be received by Mother Teresa. The time was agreed and

I was sitting on a bench near her rooms, waiting to be called, when she popped out like a sparrow, came and sat next to me, and grabbed both my hands with the words: 'God bless you, my dear.' It was so sudden and unexpected that I lost all sense of where I was. I was in the presence of a highly spiritual woman, yet I seemed to be nowhere, as in a vacuum, and had lost all thought of what I might say to her. Recovering my composure, I handed her a bunch of flowers and a donation with the promise that I would try and help her cause.* I asked if she had a message I could give to my flower ladies and she said: 'You must love one another, see the best, and smile always, for smiling is the beginning of understanding.'

The world, I feel, must already know about Mother Teresa's life and work but, when you see the sick, the poor and the dying in the streets of Calcutta, as I did, and understand her aims, you are convinced that God's finger is on her. 'I was not called,' she said, 'to be successful, but He called me to be helpful.' She told me that fifty per cent of those she picks up from the streets die, but they die happy, knowing that someone cares.

She then took me to the chapel and showed me the jewelled pendant of the Order of Merit hanging round the neck of a statue of the Virgin Mary, an award which Queen Elizabeth II had given to Mother Teresa in recognition of her work. We bowed before the statue, and I vowed to help. I watched Mother Teresa in silence as she walked away in a Chaplinesque manner – a tiny, lone figure, but she was not alone. The next morning I left for home.

*On my return to England I wrote to several NAFAS flower clubs mentioning my visit to Mother Teresa and asking for small donations. This resulted in my sending her £3,500.

22

Russia

I WAS INVITED to Russia in 1988 – a visit that was to prove a marked contrast to the one I had paid to India only a few months previously.

Of course, I was not unique in going to Russia, but with flowers? Surely, it was said, I should be taking food (which I did as well). Would I find flowers in Russia? Would what I had to say be of any value to the Russian people? Would there be snow? Would I see heavy women wrapped in shawls and headscarves clearing the roads? Where would I stay? Would I be allowed to go about on my own? We had been fed so much propaganda over the years that my trip seemed a mystery, but I was willing to discover the answer.

The USSR-Great Britain Society had asked me to give a talk and to visit a branch of the Medico-Philosophical Group. It was not made clear what the aim of the visit should be, although flowers were mentioned since they had read my books and articles. So, as flowers seem to overcome all barriers, I felt that by demonstrating with flowers, at least I could make a start.

I must have appeared a strange sight as I arrived at Moscow Airport with a huge cardboard box of flowers. I fully expected to be stopped at the customs checkpoint but was waved through as though such a box was the accepted addition to an Englishwoman's luggage.

On looking back I feel my visit was at the wrong time of the year. It was October, and there were few flowers available. In fact I was also too soon, for none of the equipment I had brought with me was available to the Russians. But it was an exploratory trip on which I was asked if I would organize an exhibition. I promised to go again the following year.

In searching out the Moscow flower scene I discovered that the well-appointed flower shops were state-owned and there was nothing, or very little, in them. I assumed that after the allotted quota from the collective farmers was sold there were no replenishments available. There was no free enterprise and no wholesale markets of flowers as we know in England; I understood the flowers were shared out equally to the shops. They all had the same. I saw people queuing for bunches of five carnations (smaller in size than ours) and was told that flowers were given as presents when visiting friends or family for special occasions, as little else, such as chocolates or cakes, was available. They are also given on name days. But what surprised me was the number of men buying flowers. In one shop there must have been about ten buckets, each containing a dozen or so carnations, some red and some pink. A number of men were strolling between the buckets picking out one here and there then taking them to the paying counter where they were charged extra if the flowers were wrapped. I watched one man choose three red carnations carefully and asked my guide to enquire for what purpose he was buying them. He answered that they were for his wife and that he bought three every week for her. They cost the equivalent of 75p each. After paying, he walked out smiling, without having them wrapped.

Russians unhesitatingly give flowers to men of rank or achievement, and flowers, ordered in advance, are given in profusion to male ballet dancers and orchestra leaders, whereas in England such an action might be thought effeminate, but I could not discover where these flowers came from. I saw no flowers in the hotels and few plants. So I made an arrangement of red gladioli, red roses and carnations for the hotel where I stayed and left it for them on their reception desk.

I was taken to the botanical gardens, where the director proudly described his plants to me which I could see were in excellent condition, but I was in search of the source of cut flowers. He then led me to an exhibition of flowers and plants but again I found it to be a plant show place with no flowers for sale. I also went to the general market where I was told I would find flowers. Here again I had to forget my idea of flower markets as we know them in the West for, tucked between other commodities, there were a only few flowers, which had been brought up from Georgia in the south (850 miles) by private growers. I wondered how economically sound it could be for these growers to travel hundreds of miles with flowers to sell but I learned that the train journeys were subsidized. In summer, these growers also bring their flowers to sell on stands outside the underground stations.

It seemed, therefore, that flowers were a luxury and were reserved for special occasions. I began to wonder if my visit could be of any use, for whereas we in England can have flowers all the year round, from our gardens, markets or imports, the Russians on the whole could not enjoy these luxuries in the state system. Nevertheless, I explained, an artistic picture could be made, even with three carnations, if a branch, or a piece of driftwood was added, even stones and dry leaves could be made to look attractive. Much interest was shown in dried flowers and herbs. I planned to take dozens of Sutton's seeds on my visit the following year.

I sensed, however, that much more was needed. Perestroika had not yet sunk in. There was more openness but the problem was the use of this new-found freedom. To believe in themselves and not to wait to be led was the answer, but it was difficult for many to accept or trust this after seventy years of submission. I discovered this for myself when I tried to give away my surplus bunches of spray carnations. The flower shop was nearly empty of flowers but a queue was still forming. I offered my flowers to the lady at the desk, but she would not take them, neither would any of the women in the queue. As I discovered later, they were nervous about being seen with more than their quota.

Still in search of flowers and their source for such occasions as weddings, I took a taxi to the Palace of Marriages. Here the brides came en masse carrying their flowers to a ceremony conducted by a registrar. No religious vows were proclaimed, but each couple was given a general talk by the registrar. The bride's flowers were presented to her by the bridegroom who ordered whatever was available well in advance. The bride also gave flowers to the groom. After the ceremony, they walked down the curved staircase of the marriage palace, which I assumed was a former aristocratic home, and then out into the open where they visited a tomb, say of Lenin, or some landmark, or just paraded for all to see and admire.

As my guide took me round Moscow, I was struck by the cleanliness of the wide streets: as children, Russians are taught to treat the streets as an extension of their homes, so no rubbish or paper is dropped. The Byzantine architecture with the gold-painted, onion-top cathedrals, at that time mostly museums, is the main attraction for visitors from the West. Inside the Kremlin walls, there are the frescoes and icons in the Cathedral of the Assumption, magnificent in their colour and portrayal of historic scenes, and the Armoury nearby which is one of their oldest museums where you can feast your eyes on examples of decorative and applied arts including crowns, gilded state carriages, precious stones and the Fabergé decorated eggs. The atmosphere as you stand and stare at these gold-topped buildings is of old Russia.

Yet in St Petersburg, until recently known as Leningrad, which I visited on both my trips to Russia, the scene seemed almost new and clinical with its clean majestic city architecture, its finely painted fabulous palaces, former homes of the tsars, its huge parks, flowerbedded in summer, and its vast symmetrical squares and graceful bridges with colossal bronze monuments – monuments larger than I had ever previously witnessed. It is here that thousands flock each year to gaze at the treasures of the past glories of Russia housed in the Halls in the Hermitage. It holds three million exhibits – art treasures from all parts of the world gathered by previous tsars, mainly Peter the Great.

You need to wander on foot to appreciate fully the magnificence of St Petersburg, the Hero City as it is called. I remember standing in awe in the great Victory Square with its tall, steel central column, which leads me to mention one of the most moving sights I have ever experienced. I refer to the memorial cemetery just outside the city where one million citizens of Leningrad, who perished during the nine-hundred-day siege (1941–1944) by the Nazis, some during air raids and shelling but mostly from starvation, are buried in mass graves. As I stood by the Eternal Flame facing the rows of tombs, at the other end of which there is a monument to the Motherland (a symbol of grief and eternal memory), the goose-stepping march of the soldiers changing the guard took place. Loudspeakers relayed the strains of 'The Dead March' from *Saul*, which charged the atmosphere with emotion. I thought of the pictures in the entrance to the cemetery of people dragging their dead on sledges to be buried only to fall victims themselves on the way back; others were buried beneath the snow in the streets as they fell. Before leaving I toured several rows of the tombs where 650,000 roses bloom in summer and where small bunches of wrapped flowers were placed. I had no flowers, but I left there part of my heart and much wonderment.

On my second visit to Russia, in 1989, everyone seemed to be more open. Visitors used to think that Russians always looked glum but my friends told me that they had learned to become faceless; they wore dull colours and did not look up or smile much for fear they might stand out when informers were near. Yet at home, within the family and with friends, Russians seemed a happy, extrovert and passionate people. I found them an emotional race unashamedly displaying trust, even by a squeeze of the hand.

It seems strange that it was seeds from the garden clubs in the USA that started me on the path of using flowers to relieve our British post-war drabness; yet there was I, forty years later, taking seeds and flowers to Russia with the same aim in mind. The wheel of life often comes full circle, and although I went to Russia with flowers, I left with love and friendship for the courageous people of that great country.

Since my last visit, my letters have gone unanswered. The situation had changed, plans put aside and Gorbachev had been overthrown. Then, surprisingly, I received an invitation to take part in an international seminar and exhibition of flower arrangement societies in Moscow in February 1992. I was intrigued for I did not know such an organization existed. I then discovered that it had been formed three years previously. I wondered if some of my words had taken root, for now there were 64 flower societies in the then Soviet Union, with five in Moscow, and they were about to stage an exhibition and five-day seminar. I concluded that they must have existed earlier in an embryonic form but had not been organized.

I went armed this time with even more flowers, fresh and dried, plus a large box of accessories, not knowing what was to be expected of me. I was soon to learn that I was speaking almost every day and demonstrating to about 750 people.

The exhibition at the Palace of the Pioneers in Moscow was good and well staged, the Russians being artistic and most imaginative. A great wave of emotion was felt as the audience rose after the demonstration amid cries of 'bravo'. They seemed to be in great need of some lift to their difficult lives.

I understood by their questions that they were in search of an identity, not being sure where they are going, so I tried to help them to believe in themselves and to trust, for there are opportunities there with flowers, if they would only strike out and not be afraid.

Perestroika now reigns but, as I noticed on my earlier visits, the Russians do not know what to do with their new-found freedom and often this leads to even more confusion. The basic requirements for daily living were still in short supply and the flower shops were often bare, although now some flowers were brought straight in from private growers to the shops without fear of the secret police watching.

It was very cold: only 5°F (15°C below zero) and grim, but by using flowers as a therapy a great warmth was engendered. I admired the courage and patience of these still-suffering people. They laugh and cry at the same time but the flower groups which came from as far afield as Vladivostock, Siberia, Estonia, Latvia, Georgia, the Caucasus and the Ukraine all seemed happy at the chance, through this 1992 exhibition, to express themselves. When travel and communication between other nations becomes more easy, they will go far with their artistic use of flowers and I thank Madame Nina Lozovaja and dear Svetlana, her interpreter, for inviting me to witness their work. I will not forget them.

27   Julia visited the Taj Mahal, near Agra, during her 1986 tour of India.

28   Here Julia chats with Mother Teresa in Calcutta, 1986.

29 Garlands of marigolds such as these are already threaded on string ready for sale in an Indian market.

30 A floor petal design on the patio of the Rambagh Palace Hotel, Jaipur. Different designs are made daily by the gardener.

31 Oncidium orchids and ferns envelop a Chinese wedding basket draped with richly embroidered Chinese silk in this exotic design from Hong Kong.

32 Here a young Thai girl shows a typical temple arrangement composed of short heads of flowers in a conical shape.

33 In this Japanese design pine and camellias are placed in a large pottery bowl in an arrangement typical of the famous Ohara school.

34 Julia greets the Princess of Wales at the opening of the 1989 Festival of Flowers in Westminster Cathedra.
Mrs Iain Ferguson, the Festival organiser, is in the background.

35 This simple design of red gladioli and red carnations was part of a lesson in Moscow in 1988, when Lenin's image was still very much in evidence.

36 Back in Moscow in 1992, Julia welcomes the snowfall outside
St Basil's Cathedral, Red Square.

PART SIX

A WORLD OF
FLOWERS

23

Here and There

THINKING OF RUSSIA and all its difficulties reminds me of my many journeys to **Beirut** before the war in 1975.

I was always delighted to meet the ladies at the Green Flower Club who were so keen on their gardens and flowers and also on working for charity. At one time their efforts were directed towards raising money for the Jewish/Arab school, for it was felt that if Jewish and Arab children grew up together there would be more tolerance between them later in life. I wonder if it helped, for the school no longer exists. Other warring factions have since brought that beautiful country to ruins.

On one of my visits the ladies took me to **Baalbek**, an ancient city north of Damascus with monumental columns and open theatres. The vastness of this site contrasted with the tiny wild flowers that struggled for survival among the dusty rocks and stones. Whilst quietly sitting on the steps of this ancient city of Baalbek, named after the Sun God, one of the women told me the following story:

One day long, long years ago, our Lord Jesus Christ was suffering, so he set out to walk in the Garden of Gethsemane. In this garden many flowers bloomed, among them a tall white flower. As Jesus passed, the flowers, realizing his pain, bowed their heads, all but one – the tall white one which stood upright. Later, as this flower realized its mistake, it began to change colour and finally, blushing to a light coral, hung its head in shame and with tears of repentance. With the spread of Christianity the flower came to Europe and was given the name crown imperial by the physician to the Duke of Florence. It was grown privately for the first time in the Imperial Gardens of Vienna.

The flower, botanically known as *Fritillaria imperialis*, is a bulbous plant which, when planted in November in England, flowers in May. It was popular with the Dutch flower painters who often placed it at the head of a group of flowers. It has tear-drop flowers hanging from a ruff of leaves.

On another visit to the **Lebanon**, to assess the work of the pupils of Mrs Lily Wilkinson, I was asked the day before judging if I would stage, for Middle East Airlines, a display of flowers that had been flown in from Ghana, then the Gold Coast. I agreed. All the other airlines that passed through Beirut were also to stage displays. A large area was marked out on the ground but, when I saw the huge quantity of flowers that were there to be used, I realized what a mammoth task I had undertaken. There were buckets full of anthuriums, strelitzias, ginger flowers, all in yellow, red and orange, orchids (*Phalaenopsis*) and masses of spiky heliconias; so many flowers that I wondered how they could all be accommodated in the space allotted me. I decided to use three tiers, the base being about nine feet and about two feet off the ground. On top of this was placed a smaller tier, with a yet smaller one at the top. The whole was covered in black sateen. Beaten copper vessels, some small, some large, were obtained on loan from shops. With no one to help me, I worked for hours placing four large arrangements at each corner of the lower tier with small arrangements in between. Similar designs were on the layer above this, with a large copper urn at the top filled with heliconias. I was pleased with the result.

Next morning was to be the judging, then sadly, we learned that there had been a MEA crash with many casualties. The directors decided that all the flowers were to be removed from display, with the exception of the large arrangement at the top of this black, shrouded structure. The flowers, alas, were not seen by the public.

Remembering my trip to the Lebanon and the legend of the crown imperial made me think of the time I was judging in **Bermuda**. There I was given a waxed passion flower wrapped in cotton wool in a box ready for travelling. Apparently these curious climbing blooms grow more profusely there than in England and an enterprising lady preserves them by dipping each flower into hot wax then plunging it into iced water. These are then on sale to visitors. Later, when I met this lady, she was pleased to hear from me the legend of her favourite flower.

It appears that after the victorious campaign by the Jesuits in the sixteenth century in South America, they sought a favourable omen. They found it in a scrambling plant by the seashore which they called passion flower. The ten creamy-white outside petals represented, for these men, the ten faithful apostles (Judas and Doubting Thomas were apparently omitted). The outer corona represents the numerous disciples, and the inner corona the Crown of Thorns. The five stamens represent Christ's five wounds and the three-part stigma the nails. The curling tendrils represent the cords with which our Lord was whipped and bound, and the five-part leaves are a reminder of the clutching hands of the soldiers. When the Jesuits found the natives feasting on the yellow pear-shaped fruits, which appear following the flowers, it seemed a sign that the Indians were thirsting for Christianity and that Christianity would be the religion of this new-found world.

I also remember another legend, which concerns the story of the poinsettia, known in **Mexico** as the *flor de la Nochebuena*, or the flower of the Nativity:

It was Christmas Eve and music resounded in the village streets of Monterey in Mexico. Maria was poor and she became sad as she watched all the villagers pass her on their way to the church with their presents for the Christ Child. She had no present, but ran into the house and picked up a cup thinking she would take that as it was so beautiful. As she ran to catch up with the others she fell and broke the cup, which made her even more sad, for now she had nothing.

As she sat by the roadside she noticed a plant.* She would take that, she thought, for even the humblest offering, if given with love, is beautiful in His sight. She ran up the hill and was breathless as she entered the church, dazzling bright with the light which flooded the crib. She knelt and laid her gift on the altar murmuring: 'With all my love.' Then, as she left to go, the lights seemed to become brighter and brighter, and she noticed that her flower was beginning to turn a bright red, and others knelt in amazement at the miraculous change of the humble offering, which afterwards became known as the flower of the Nativity.

Thirty years ago flowers also took me to that lovely island in the Mediterranean called **Malta**. I was to give daily lessons to the women who were forming the Malta Flower Club in the large basement garage of Rosaleen Weldon's home. Today they have their own premises in a splendid house with a lecture room. In May 1991, they staged a magnificent flower festival in the cathedral of the ancient city of Mdina, which must surely have been one of the best I have ever witnessed, in spite of Malta's lack of indigenous vegetation. Whoever said that Malta was the biggest heap of rubble he had ever seen had obviously not looked behind the walls that surround the houses and their gardens on this island.

Flowers and plants have so much to tell us that I am always intrigued to come across plants I have not seen before, so when I spotted hundreds of tall, thin trees growing on the mountainsides and slopes of the ravines in **Bali**, I asked what they were. They are nutmeg trees (*Myristica fragrans*), I was told, and I immediately thought of a friend who always carried a nutmeg in his pocket to ward off rheumatism. When doing some flowers in the Sanur Beach Hotel, the manager told me that although he had not heard about carrying a nutmeg, it was well known that if nutmegs, clove and a type of dried chilli are fried in coconut oil and then ground, the resulting paste is a sure cure if rubbed into the body at night.

The manager also told me that when a baby is born in Bali, the placenta is buried in the garden, so that even if a Balinese travels away from home, he always returns. 'That is why,' he added, 'you do not see the Balinese settling in foreign cities owning restaurants, as the Chinese do.' He looked at me quizzically, then whispered, as if for my ears only, that nutmeg was a good aphrodisiac used in no matter what form.

A visit to **Cyprus**, where I was to demonstrate to the members of the flower club, was also memorable. The red gladioli I had requested were in tight bud hardly showing any colour and I needed red for my motif. Grasping the bunch, I explained to the president, Mrs Asdig Shekerdemian, that I knew how to get them open. I recut and slit the stems and stood them in warm water with a little sugar, then, against the president's advice, I stood them outside in the sun saying that should do the trick. Half an hour later I went to investigate, only to find that they were all shrivelled up. I had not reckoned with the harsh heat of the Cyprus sunshine, but the incident taught me not to think always that I know.

However, when I was in what was then **West Germany** not long after the Second World War, my flowers would not open because of the cold. I was on a tour of sixteen Royal Air Force stations, the object being for me to relieve the boredom of the service wives. They had no option but to buy from the NAAFI shop: all their furnishings were of the same design, they wore similar clothes and many were complaining of the lack of variety. My brief was to go from station to station encouraging the ladies to open their eyes to the natural world around them, explaining how to brighten their homes by making designs with branches and fir cones when flowers were unobtainable.

Apparently the army officials were envious of this airforce venture so, at the end of my trip, I presented a demonstration to all the army wives. This was a voluntary job and I enjoyed it but whether I succeeded in my aims I never knew. Today, however, there are flourishing flower clubs among wives of servicemen in that part of Germany, many of the members being very talented and providing most of the flower decorations needed on all the special occasions.

Writing of this excursion in Germany, of wartime difficulties, and post-war problems in Europe, brings me to an unusual journey to **Czechoslovakia** in 1968 when Mr Alexander Dubček, as president, was trying to introduce a little more freedom to that country.

I was invited to arrange flowers in Bohemian glass for a photographic calendar, which was to be sent to all their overseas agents. The world-famous Bohemian glassware was one industry the Russians had allowed Czechoslovakia to keep all others had been turned over to heavy industry.

I flew out on a Czech plane and was driven from Prague airport to Liberec in the north where the glass was made. I could choose any item I wanted from the showroom in the great Palace of Glass, but was shocked when I met the photographer, who had only one type of film, no background material and only one light. He was a sensitive and artistic man who knew exactly what he would like to do but was not given the means to carry out his work. I was taken to the local park for flowers; there was not much choice but we managed to make some interesting pictures.

The state of the town, my hotel and the streets was depressing: no paint, rusty pipes in rooms, broken pavements, holes in the road, nothing in the shops, people covered but hardly 'dressed'. Coming as it did twenty years before my Russian trip I was saddened by this, my first, sight of a communist-run country.

I returned to Liberec the next year with a large box of flowers but by now Mr Dubček had been deposed and some of the people I had met previously had 'died of heart attacks'. I was moved on to Olomouc where there is a famous annual flower show which attracts thousands. I demonstrated at this show, my arrangements in Bohemian glass being left as part of the decor.

At the end of the show I was presented with a glass goblet engraved with the Lidice Rose. For those who do not know the story, Lidice was a village of seven thousand inhabitants in Bohemia which was razed to the ground by the Nazis in reprisal for the assassination of Reinhard Heydrich, the so-called German 'Protector' of Bohemia. All the men of the village were lined up by a wall and shot, and the women and children were sent to separate labour camps, some never to meet again. Not a sign of anything living was left . . . no tree, no house, no shop. How tragic are the results of war; one wonders where the survivors are now. Today, Lidice is a park with a Memorial Rose Garden.

When I travelled through the country I was able to reach the hearts of the people and to learn of their problems. For instance, joining a long line of motorists waiting for petrol from a dull-green painted pump at the side of the road, I suggested we went on to another, rather than wait. 'But there is no other,' it was explained, 'there is no competition, and we know where the state tanks are placed. If we do not get it here there will not be another for many miles.'

I am still in touch with my Czech friends and often send them flower books but never know whether they arrive.

However, on to better and more recent times. **Spain** is a country I had always longed to explore. I started to learn Spanish once with this in mind, but somehow Spain never came the way of my work until I was asked to speak at the inaugural meeting of the Costa Blanca Flower Club in 1984. Mrs Mary Carpenter, a new resident near Alicante, had initiated this club with the aim of serving the English-speaking community on the south-east coast of Spain.

The meeting was a great success and the club continues to flourish. Like most flower arrangers, I collected all kinds of unusual plant material, such as racemes of pepper pods, palm leaves and strands of date beans. All these items were packed in a box for my use in photography when I returned home. On the plane the stewardess stowed my box behind some seats at the back and I joined a fellow passenger who was alone and very chatty. Halfway on our journey she became unwell; the stewardesses helped and, on landing, I promised to stay with her until she could find her relatives. Concerned with getting her off the plane and across the tarmac, I completely forgot my box of plant goodies and another scheme for photography had to be devised.

Anyone who has stood in that great square in **Marakesh** listening to the storytellers could not have failed to be affected by the pungent scents coming from the stalls around the perimeter. Huge sacks containing rosebuds ready to be scooped up, like flour, stood at the side of the stalls. Powdered mixtures of mint, bay, nutmeg and cloves could be weighed at your command and all kinds of aromatic oils are wafted before your nose as you gaze. One stallholder offered me a small phial of flower oil adding that it would make my body beautiful. Realizing the cost of the phial and acknowledging my dry skin, I felt it would prove too costly to cover my body with it. Remembering my mother's adage that what is seen on the outside comes from within, I felt I had better stick to taking my cod-liver oil.

Still on flowers and their essences, I have always subscribed to the flower medicine of Dr Edward Bach. A highly skilled physician, he left his remunerative Harley Street practice to devote his time to proving his theory that many illnesses are caused through the mind. His little book *The Twelve Healers* is a good starting point to his work but to find out more about this remarkable man, there is a book entitled *The Medical Discoveries of Dr Edward Bach* by Nora Weeks.**

Sitting at lunch one day next to Gerard van der Kemp, formerly the curator of the Palace of Versailles, I was issued with an invitation to visit **Giverny**, the house and garden of the artist, Monet. I had longed to see this garden, the subject of so many of his paintings. So, after judging at a recent International Floral Art Show in Versailles, I made my way out of Paris to the village of Giverny in Normandy.

The garden was a dream; chaotic yet with some kind of order, just as I love to see a garden, with blousy paeonies drooping over pathways and roses tumbling from archways. Ferns and foxgloves (*Digitalis*) tried to hide themselves in a shady corner, whilst deutzias and escallonias tumbled over fences and gateways. There was a riot of colour, though no harsh colours, with flowers growing in abandon everywhere. Everywhere that is, until I walked through a tunnel and reached the stillness of the lakes. I imagined Monet sitting here beside his easel painting the scenes in front of him: wistaria-covered bridges, weeping willows hanging over the water under which can be discerned a small rowing boat amid the water irises and feathery astilbes.

There was a scene for a painting at every step and I found it difficult to tear myself away from this magical garden to the point that I spent little time in the house, which had been restored with funds from a trust for which Mr van der Kemp had worked so hard. The garden is a gem and should be visited by all flower and garden lovers.

Not too far away is the village of **Fiacre** in Brittany and, as so many people confuse St Francis of Assisi, the patron saint of nature, with St Fiacre the patron saint of gardeners, I made my way there to authenticate the story of the gardeners' saint which happened a long time ago:

About AD 670, there was a young boy named Fiachra, who lived in Ireland. He loved the green fields and plants and would talk to them by name. Sadly he was often kept inside the walls of his father's castle because the pagans were always fighting.

As he grew older he became tired of the constant battles and decided to leave and make his way to a monastery in Brittany about which a holy man had told him, for there he felt he could find peace. He first made a boat and sailed away. Then, after reaching the French coast, he walked and walked until at last he reached the monastery. He explained that he did not mind what work he was given to do as long as he could stay so, to test his sincerity, the father told him to go into the woods and mark out as much land as he could in one day. He must then learn to live off it and to build a house. This he did and, in order to grow food, he dug and sowed seeds.

He loved his garden and blessed it each night and day and the more he worked with God's help, the more his garden grew. People heard about this lovely garden and many came to see it. Fiachra, whose name was now changed to Fiacre, blessed them all and gave them the fruits of his garden. Some, when they arrived, were sick and dispirited, but they all left refreshed and happy.

Fiacre lived alone, worked hard and studied hard. Over a number of years he cured many people with his garden herbs and kindly nature. He never saw his parents again and, after a long life, he died a happy man. Stories of his garden and his work grew and hundreds of years later he was made a saint.

The beautiful chapel of St Fiacre was built in 1480 in the Flamboyant Gothic style. Today you can visit it on the Quimper road in Brittany, as I did. But, alas, his garden is no more.

You may wonder what all this has to do with flower arranging, but just as devotees of any other interest or hobby discover further aspects when travelling, so also do flower arrangers.

For me there was an unexpected development when I demonstrated in **Maryland**, USA, in 1975. I noticed the newspapers were full of the story of the first American woman to be made a saint. Her name was Elizabeth Ann Seton (1774–1821), daughter of a distinguished English-born doctor, Richard Bayley, and widow of William Seton, grandson of Sir William Seton, a devoted adherent of Mary Queen of Scots and comptroller of Scottish Revenues.

I had read in family books of the Seton colleges in the USA and of the Seton Sisters of Charity. As Seton is my married name, and since I was so near Emmitsburg in Maryland, where the first school was founded, I investigated further. I made the pilgrimage to St Joseph's and placed flowers near the cross where Mother Elizabeth Ann Seton was buried. There was great excitement as she was to be canonized that very September, 1975, for her life's devotion to the poor and needy, for founding an orphanage as well as the Sisters of Charity, and for the proven miracles she had performed or were performed through her. A splendid statue in blue stone of Saint Elizabeth Seton can now be seen in St Patrick's Cathedral on Fifth Avenue in New York.

I mention this episode not only for the significance of a great religious event which took place in the Basilica of St Peter in Rome, to which I was invited, but also, in a distant way, for Saint Elizabeth's connection with flowers and horticulture. Her husband's father, also William Seton, had at the age of seventeen emigrated to America armed only with his good name and a letter of introduction to Richard Curzon, of the aristocratic Curzons of Waterperry, near Oxford, England, and whose daughter, Rebecca, he married in New York in 1767.

The estate of Waterperry later became a horticultural college and anyone who visited the Chelsea Flower Show until a few years ago will remember Miss Havergal and her famous display of strawberries from Waterperry that invariably won a Gold Medal. The house is now a philosophical centre which I often attend but the historic church in the grounds, with its Curzon brasses and the famous ornamental gardens, are now open to the public.

So it was flowers that took me to Maryland but also brought me to learn another passage in the history of the historic Seton family, who had harboured Mary Queen of Scots and, as Jacobites, fought and lost against Queen Elizabeth I.

It seems that no matter where I have found myself, flowers have opened doors to wonderful experiences and friendships. Bus conductors and taxi drivers in England will always chat when I'm carrying flowers, telling me of the varieties they grow and of their special interests. Eyes light up when I talk of flowers in every country I have visited. Although economists and politicians help the world go round, flowers can also play a powerful part.

---

*The roadside plant could have been the common euphorbia, for our present-day poinsettia is *Euphorbia pulcherrima*, the bright red bracts being brought into colour in glasshouses by strong, constant overhead light.
**Both books were published by C W Daniel Co Ltd in 1933 and 1940 respectively.

24

Here at Home

READING BOOKS on the Seton family during moments at home brings to mind how many people ask me what I actually do here. I am totally involved in my work and do not lead a great social life. To some this may sound dull but my work is so absorbing, so varied, so never-ending in interest, that I thank the good Lord each day that I have found my vocation.

In between journeys abroad, I judge flower shows all over the country, and there are many of them, for almost every village and town in Britain holds annual flower shows; it is a way of life. In addition, many big shows are held: in Birmingham, Harrogate, Liverpool, Shrewsbury, Southport and London, plus shows staged by city organizations such as banks and insurance companies. All of these, as well as NAFAS, club and area shows, attract thousands of visitors, for few in England can resist the call of a flower show in case a new style or discovery in some plant form is to be seen.

The show that is the highlight of my year is the Chelsea Flower Show. I have judged the decorative arrangements every year since the Second World War and this magnificent show is still magic to me. I become excited as I watch those huge marquees being erected about three weeks before the event and I cannot bear to leave the scene even after it is closed.

The show is staged by the Royal Horticultural Society (RHS), which was formed in 1804 and granted a royal charter by Queen Victoria in 1861. It was first held in the Temple gardens in May 1888 but was transferred to the Royal Hospital grounds in Chelsea in 1913. It is the world's most prestigious flower show, attracting exhibitors from all corners of the earth.

Staged as it is by the RHS, a learned society, the show is designed not so much as a spectacle, although it is one, as an educational exposition, where almost every plant in the world is exhibited for the benefit of the public, who may ask questions of the exhibitors and obtain an expert reply.

The Queen and members of the royal family annually attend a private viewing on the day before the official opening. Until 1988 it was estimated that about 250,000 people visited the show during its four days' duration. In 1988 a limit was set to reduce the number to 190,000 for the visitors' own comfort and safety. It is one of the most democratic meeting places where the lord of the manor and the gardener meet on an equal level to discuss the value of the plants and flowers.

Unlike the great exhibition centres at Olympia and Earls Court in London, and in Birmingham, which are under cover and have permanent facilities for the public, such as catering and toilets, the Chelsea Flower Show is held in a public park which is normally covered with grass, trees, ornamental shrubs and roadways. The three-and-a-half-acre Great Marquee is the largest in the world (authenticated in the *Guinness Book of Records*) and the contract for erecting it has been held by Piggot Brothers of Ongar, Essex, since 1912. Founded in 1780 the firm is known to have supplied tents to the opposing armies in the American Civil War.

The atmosphere within the marquee, with its dazzling displays of flowers, and perfumed air, seems to transport visitors into a magical land of brilliant colours and foliage. There are roses in profusion with new varieties and unusual colours as well as the more familiar favourites. There are beautiful clematis, in urns and climbing up trellises, some with blooms the size of small saucers, upright lupins standing stiff as soldiers, giant delphiniums, some eight feet tall, in all shades of blue, a few pale lemon, and now some in red. Paeonies in all varieties and colours, carnations, poppies, and highly scented sweet peas are there to titillate the senses. You can see banks of orchids, sometimes clinging from trees as in the jungle. It all becomes a little heady as you stroll around passing huge displays of tulips and daffodils on the way. Some flowers need forcing to be at their best in May, others have to be held back in cold storage. It all seems a miracle, especially when you see delicate wild flowers growing round pseudo-cottages and yet, nearby, you can gaze on proteas from South Africa arranged to almost reach the top of the marquee, and wax-like anthuriums, with other exotics, from Barbados. Unusual strelitzias and heliconias come from Trinidad to take their place among the typically English flowering shrubs such as lilacs, philadelphus, deutzias, escallonias and annual flowers that bloom in perfection on undulating banks.

The superbly designed outside gardens with their fountains, pools, bridges, sun houses and rock gardens, are there to be bought or to be copied and ideas for gardens, patios, hanging baskets and window boxes abound for all to take note of – pencil and notebook are a must when walking round. Nothing is omitted, from garden machinery to small or lavish conservatories and every kind of garden accessory, including books and magazines, is available.

The Chelsea Flower Show is a gardener's world. You can ask questions of experts, send flowers by Teleflorist and Interflora to any part of the world, or order your party flower decorations from the famous decorators who display their artistry.

The amateur flower arrangers are also there in force, but it was not always so. I remember travelling on the *Queen Elizabeth* in February 1947 on my way to the International Flower Show in New York, and discussing with the then Lord Aberconway, a fellow passenger who was to be principal guest at the show, the future of Britain's gardens after the years of neglect during the Second World War. He was then president of the Royal Horticultural Society. Later, after the opening of the New York show, we both stood in amazement before the illuminated niches displaying what were surely works of art from the flower-arrangement classes. Accustomed as we were in Britain to seeing large, symmetrical bowls of perfectly grown flowers without backgrounds, it was certainly exciting to see linear-patterned designs comprising perhaps a twig, or only five flowers, which were not even grown by the exhibitor. Lord Aberconway wondered if such staged exhibits could be shown at our own Chelsea Flower Show, and some readers might remember those electric-lighted niches at Chelsea in 1948. The innovation lasted only one year for many passed by this section on their way to their favourite plant exhibits, without appreciating the significance of floral art. To me, however, these arrangements seemed even more lovely than those I had seen in the USA, for the plant material used was rarer and more varied and had been grown by the exhibitor. It quickly became evident all over the country that the former idea of the 'Bowl, arranged for effect' was not enough for our post-war women who were hungry for some new form of self-expression.

At most pre-1939 shows it was nearly always the silver bowl, full of the most glorious flowers picked by the person with the largest garden, which won the first prize, judged by gardeners. I now wanted everyone to have a chance and so introduced 'An arrangement of five flowers, with any foliage'. No account was taken of the intrinsic value of the container – bottles, dishes and other household items could be used. These classes were eventually evaluated by floral-art judges.

Today, in comparison with those earlier years, the exhibits are staged with great artistry and, although at first it was difficult to obtain the permission of the authorities for flower arrangements to be included (some felt they might appear too frivolous), they are now a great feature of the Chelsea Flower Show. The members of NAFAS are responsible for one great island exhibit in the main marquee, whilst club members display their artistry to a theme in a special flower-arrangement tent. Britain's top professional florists also have their own section in the main marquee, where there are flowers designed for every occasion. All of this is covered in detail by the media.

Living nearby, I watch all these activities as though I belong, and even after the event, I watch the turf being restored to its former glory. I see the show gardens being dug up, the shops being demolished, the hanging baskets removed and the great marquee being dismantled. I walk through this almost barren area, stooping now and again to pick up a fallen flower. It is all over for another year.

Another great show that is a significant date in my home calendar is the great Rose Festival staged by the Royal National Rose Society at their own grounds at St Albans. In addition to judging at this show, a visit gives me the opportunity of seeing one of the most comprehensive assemblies of roses anywhere in the world. About 30,000 roses of all varieties are there to be shared. They climb up and over the pergolas by the lake, they clamber up trees and the low-growing ground-cover ones have their own beds close to the named hybrid tea roses. These modern roses vie with the old-fashioned roses, which have a special area to themselves. In fact, during show days you seldom have time to investigate all that is happening in the 21 or more acres that constitute the society's grounds.

The festival is held in July, the commercial exhibits of roses being laid out artistically with the amateur exhibits in a marquee of their own. Everyone there grows or loves roses. I, for one, become intoxicated each time I attend not only by the beauty and scent of the roses, but also by the atmosphere and fresh smell of crushed grass as the thousands of people walk over it in their enthusiasm for the rose.

Writing of roses, I feel I must mention another annual event which I often attend. This is the Knollys' Rose Ceremony that takes place on Midsummer Day. A descendant of Sir Robert Knollys picks a rose from a City garden to present to the Lord Mayor of London as a quit rent. The rose is an annual fine for a misdemeanour which Lady Knollys committed in 1481. For nearly six hundred years this annual ceremony has taken place. How did it all start?

Sir Robert Knollys was not only a friend of the Black Prince, but also fought beside him in the Battle of Crécy in 1346. He became the country's most famous soldier, so when he retired from the French Wars in 1381 to a small house in Seething Lane in the City of London, his proud wife bought a second house on the opposite side of the narrow lane and built a little footbridge over the road to connect the two. She asked no permission to do this and paid no attention to the by-laws, for who dare criticize, she argued, when she was only providing a dignified background in the crowded City for the country's greatest soldier.

But she forgot that London had a lord mayor and corporation, and her act caused them great concern. Should they overlook it? Or would this give her free rein for further ideas? They finally held a private session and decided they must impose a fine. On being approached, not as a soldier but as a citizen, Sir Robert said he well understood their attitude and was prepared to give up a year of his pension, or whatever was decided, as a common-law fine.

Surprised by his attitude, some of the aldermen felt the matter should be dismissed. Others felt that this connivance would induce chaos, so reference was made to the pages of old Guildhall records.

Peppercorn rent as a fine had often been demanded, but as peppercorns were seldom found on English soil, they decided that something utterly English – a rose, plucked fresh each year from Sir Robert's garden in Seething Lane – should be paid as quit rent for the footbridge that had been built without obtaining the right. In the early days Sir Robert rode wearing full military uniform to present to the mayor his rose, carried on a cushion, and previously blessed at All Hallows' Church.

Today the rose is cut from the same garden in Seething Lane and is carried in procession by the churchwardens of All Hallows, who hand it over to the family's representative who, in turn, presents it to the Lord Mayor. As I stood there on a recent Midsummer Day, a fellow guest asked me what it signified now. I explained that it meant that civil authority was then, and still is, the true source of our common life. Military status was not even then supreme over the common law, but subject to it. This was, and is, the basis of our ordered freedom, perfectly illustrated by the ceremony of Knollys' Rose.

Writing consumes much of my time, for I write up most of these shows and events for the press. Then I spend time also with photographers and there is also television. I speak at luncheons and dinners, open shows, present prizes and attend the meetings and conferences of the Women's Institutes, which first gave me a platform. Private gardens, too, I always enjoy visiting. I also demonstrate in hospitals and prisons. Once I volunteered to speak to the women in a hospital for the mentally ill, hoping to open their eyes to the beauty that was around them in the gardens. I was asked to speak very simply as many patients were under drugs. I explained how a picture could be made with flowers by putting different shapes and sizes together, adding anything they cared to find even stones or shells. I repeated this idea several times in order to emphasize my message to them until, in the middle of my talk, one patient stood up and shouted: 'That's all balderdash, it's a lot of rubbish.' She was taken out by the matron who later apologized: 'We were very sorry for you, but were delighted ourselves, for that was the first time that woman had spoken in two years.'

The purpose of my demonstration in a large women's prison was to lift morale. I felt this would be difficult for I could hardly tell prisoners what they could do with a few flowers the next week, month or year, if they were going to be there for a long time, so I asked the wardress for guidance, only to be told that I would have to find my own way. So I spoke to them not only about flower arranging but encouraged them to open their eyes to nature. It went very well and on the way out I said to the wardress that I had not found the experience half as terrifying as I thought it was going to be and that I thought the prisoners looked happy in their grey and white uniforms. I added that I liked the uniform with the red ties best and asked why they didn't all wear ties. 'Oh,' replied the wardress. 'They're the second offenders.'

Most of my articles for magazines and newspapers are illustrated and my books include fifty or more photographs of flower arrangements. When working on *Flower Arrangements for Stately Homes**, I was invited to photograph the flowers in Sutton Place, the home of the late J Paul Getty. He asked that I only use flowers picked from the garden which seemed to be full of daffodils. I chose the long Spanish-oak table on which to place my flowers below the magnificent Rubens oil painting, *Diana and Her Nymphs*. I would have preferred to use larger, more exotic flowers, perhaps lilies, below this grand picture, but kept faith with Mr Getty's request. Halfway through the arrangement, he popped his head round a side door and said: 'Now young lady, don't you start putting flowers in front of my painting.' I replied that as the painting was 32 feet high and his daffodils were only 18 inches he need not worry. With that he withdrew, closed the door, and I did not see him again.

When photographing in stately homes, there was always a problem between the head gardener and the butler. The gardener wanted the most choice flowers kept in the greenhouse in order that they could be seen there by his lordship, whereas the butler wanted them in the house to be admired by visitors in the drawing-room. I often fell between the two. Once, after having been invited by Lady Zia Wernher to photograph at her home, she told me over lunch that I was not allowed to pick any flowers from the garden as the Queen was to be a weekend guest and she wanted to see the garden. Thanks to the patience of the photographer, who was sent to the servants' quarters for lunch whilst I lunched with Lady Zia, it all ended well. Photographers all seem to have endless patience. It must be one of their necessary qualities for success.

Before the advent of local radio, and in the early days of colour television, I was often called upon to perform, as flowers showed up so well in colour. When doing a weekly series entitled *It's an Idea*, I had to present a fresh idea at every session; the difference could lie in the vase, the flowers, the style or the event. One day I chose to show how to make a vase from a melted gramophone record. In order to shape the record it had to be submerged in hot water to make it pliable. During rehearsals it failed as the water was not hot enough. Later when appearing live, however, the water was so hot that I could not insert my hands in it and the record dropped to the bottom of the bowl. With one finger I hooked it out, then moulded it into an attractive shape ready for the flowers, but the next day I had a very swollen and blistered forefinger.

One charity luncheon that I am involved with started on an unknown note but has now become a great success. This is the Floral Luncheon held each year at The Savoy Hotel in aid of the Forces Help Society. I have organized the flower-arrangement exhibition that precedes the luncheon for the past thirty-five years, yet it nearly did not happen in the first place. Although Sir David Bowes-Lyon, was to be president with the Marchioness of Salisbury as chairman, we had sold only half the amount of tickets required and were considering cancelling the event. I then wrote a short article for the *Daily Telegraph* on 'How to keep your cut flowers living longer', with special reference to lilac so popular in May at the time of the luncheon. Interwoven with this advice I mentioned the charity Floral Luncheon. This resulted in another two hundred tickets being sold. So successful was this first event that we opened our next Floral Luncheon the following year with a waiting list for tickets and, despite inflation, rising costs and the increase in the price of tickets, we have been sold out annually ever since. The luncheon, a stylish affair, has almost become the opening of the London season.

Through this luncheon we have been able to raise £250,000 over the past thirty-three years, funds that have been desperately needed to keep the work of the Society going. Indeed, with continuing wars in various parts of the world, including Northern Ireland, the demands on the Society's workshops and homes for the disabled have increased.

The raising of money is not easy, but in our case it has been a team effort by our distinguished presidents and chairmen who, by their warm and sincere persuasion, have elicited generous support. Famous speakers at the luncheon have included: Jeffrey Archer, Cecil Beaton, Lord Carrington, Barbara Cartland, Moira Lister, Norman St John Stevas, Margaret Thatcher, Lord Tonypandy and Lord Whitelaw. Flowers have been sent to us by organizations from all over the world and my innumerable flower friends have unstintingly responded with their flowers, skills and time to create the superb displays that have been such an attraction at these luncheons.

I am involved with many other charitable events and my corres-pondence is vast for I enjoy hearing from flower arrangers from all over the world. As Life Vice-President of the National Association of Flower Arrangement Societies (NAFAS) and president or patron of other societies, I am happy to take part in many of their events includ-ing the decoration for church flower festivals. These festivals are popular with a great many people, including overseas visitors, espec-ially when they take place in such historic settings as St Paul's Cathe-dral, Westminster Cathedral, Westminster Abbey, Wells Cathedral and York Minster. The funds raised go towards restoring the fabric of these great edifices. Similarly, many of England's stately homes have been the setting for flower festivals, which have been staged to help cover the high costs of taxation and death duties on these splendid houses. To make these events authentic, I have studied their paintings, furniture and history and sometimes I have myself escorted groups of garden lovers round these historic houses and gardens of England, where so much can be learnt on the spot.

Of my own visits to private gardens, the ones to see Beverley Nichols's stands out in my memory. He invited me one day to lunch and to see his new garden extension in which, among other plants, he had grown some Japanese decorative cabbages. As we walked around he pointed out each flower as a friend that he knew and loved. Even the simple ones had his full attention as the following poem, 'A Bluebell', included in what he termed his first and last book of poems, *Twilight*,** proves:

> It was no doubt absurd
> That I went back again
> Against the driving rain
> To fetch this solitary flower that had been left
> When I had picked the others
> But I'd sensed that it would feel bereft
> Deserted by its brothers
> To droop beneath the copper beech
> Whilst they were sheltered in a bowl
> Safe from the fury of the wind and weather,
> No doubt I was a fool.
> Flowers, you may say, can have no soul,
> Besides, this modest bloom, so pale and weak
> Hung on a withered stalk
> With but an hour or two to live:
> And yet, had it the power of speech
> I do believe it would beseech
> That I'd not leave it there to die alone.
>
> For those who have a grain of commonsense,
> How foolish this will seem!
> I hope there is some recompense
> For those who dream this sort of dream.

Beverley Nichols loved everything that grew and writing about flowers and plants was his business. I was greatly saddened when he died but kept a special memory of my last visit to him in hospital, when taking him champagne. Expecting to find him at death's door, I discovered him instead sitting in a chair in a silk dressing gown drinking gin and tonic. 'I'm sorry I cannot offer you any Julia,' he said, 'for I had to bribe the nurse to get me this one.'

I have often been asked why I did not go into business at the height of the interest in floral art. I suppose it was because I simply did not want to, for I certainly had many opportunities. In addition to a West End shop in London, I was asked to put my name to a string of businesses all over the country. However, I felt that looking after these enterprises would demand too much of my time and energy and I needed to be free to go out and talk to people. I was never interested in making money for myself. I am rich in health, friends and spirit and that is sufficient.

In the Queen's New Year's Honours List of 1989, I was awarded the Order of the British Empire and went to Buckingham Palace to receive the insignia.

Arriving early, I was ushered into the entrance hall. I then walked up the grand, red-carpeted staircase where members of the dismounted Household Cavalry in full-dress uniform stood motionless at every corner. Along the corridors, their glittering white-plumed helmets, red jackets and shiny black jackboots vied in splendour with the portraits on the embossed silk walls. I wished for more time to study these portraits which, unlike those in public galleries, are untitled. With others who were to receive awards, I was shown into a room where instructions were given to us. Then, ten at a time in alphabetical order, we were taken to the entrance to the magnificent red and gold ball-room where we could see the preceding recipients going through their paces. My eyes fell on a shallow bowl of planted spring flowers on a side table where I stood waiting to be called. There were hyacinths, polyanthus, snowdrops, miniature tulips and ivy – they struck such a simple and refreshing note in the pomp that was taking place. My name was called. I went forward and curtsied to the Queen, who was wearing a dress the colour of crushed strawberries and looking very lovely. She was flanked on either side by two Yeomen of the Guard, members of Britain's oldest regiment. She then asked what my work was. I did not expect this but answered: 'Flowers, I try to help people find themselves through flowers.' 'And what a good idea,' she replied. I then took four paces backwards and curtsied again as I left, with the soft strains of the orchestra ringing in my ears. Photographs and a champagne lunch with the family followed. It was a wonderful experience that I felt recognized the work of all flower arrangers.

*Published by George Newnes in 1966.
**Published by Bachman & Turner in 1982.

25
NAFAS

T HE READER will be aware that my life is entwined with the National Association of Flower Arrangement Societies of Great Britain (NAFAS).

After the Second World War, with the rapidly increasing interest in flower arranging, it was obvious that some official organization would have to be formed. Flower clubs were springing up all over the country and it was an exciting time for women, who craved some form of expression. In 1950 I had a six- by three-foot map of Great Britain in my Chelsea studio into which I stuck a black-headed pin at each place where I spoke and where I thought there was potential for a club. Leaflets and encouragement followed every visit.

But it was running too quickly. Where were the speakers, the demonstrators and the teachers to be found? I described in Part One how I gave the first course for judges in 1952, beginning a monthly newsletter in 1953 to keep everyone in touch. But we were floundering until in 1959, with the initial help and advice of the Royal Horticultural Society, NAFAS was formed with Mrs Cecil Pope as its first president. Many dedicated ladies had fought hard to bring this about much to the joy of all those who have followed. For myself, I did not seek an administrative post. I needed to be free to carry on with my crusade of encouraging people wherever I was called.

However, with a full heart I would like to record my admiration and praise for the fine work these pioneers have done in forming the association that has furthered the love and use of flowers and gardens.

Today there are more than 1,300 clubs with over 100,000 members in twenty areas, all affiliated to the national organization. The officers continue to work hard to interest and help their members, who all now have a chance to exhibit their artistic skills at shows and exhibitions. They are also given the opportunity to decorate stately homes, churches and other famous edifices for charity; to date they have raised more than four million pounds. NAFAS has developed a sense of service among the members, many of whom, in their turn, go out to teach, speak and demonstrate to others.

Clubs have twinned with their counterparts in other nations, exchanging ideas for shows, information on plants and conservation. In 1982 a World Association of Flower Arrangers was formed in Great Britain to link all those in other lands with similar interests. Who knows what further horizons have to be uncovered but, for those in this country interested in making a start, you have only to write to the National Association of Flower Arrangement Societies, 21a Denbigh Street, London SW1V 2HF, England. Ask for the address of a club in your district and, if one does not exist near to you or in your country, why not form one – for that is how the pioneers started.

26

What Has It All Achieved?

WHEN FIRST DISCUSSING the idea of *My Life With Flowers*, my publisher asked me what I thought my work had achieved. It made me think back over the many years since my start and I wondered how I could possibly assess not only the present, but the long-term effects of my early efforts.

I know that making a picture with living flowers has led many people to be more aware of nature and of living things. It has provided a creative outlet for many who do not have the time to pursue the study of other arts. Flowers are readily available whether you have a large or small garden, or none at all, for there is always the countryside or a nearby shop. Whatever you want to do, for no matter what occasion, you can see the result almost at once.

Flower arranging has led many into the study of horticulture, for just as a couturier has to understand his fabrics and an artist his paints and brushes, so also does a flower arranger have to understand flowers, their durability and flexibility in use. Decorating with flowers is an ephemeral art. What is done one week is not there the next and so it presents a constant challenge.

It has helped people, particularly women, to find themselves, to open their eyes. It has led them to the study of history and architecture and to look at decorated china, pottery and paintings. For in decorating our churches, cathedrals, stately homes and other historic buildings with flowers, a knowledge of background needs to be acquired. I am convinced it has been of great benefit to tens of thousands of people not only in the home but wherever they are called upon to demonstrate their skills. An art, born of necessity when nothing else but flowers was available, has created a new world of friendship, and I am deeply grateful to all those who have provided me with a platform from which to voice my beliefs.

For my own part, it has enriched my life for I had not found my

186

way until I discovered flowers. I have often wondered if they may have a greater role to play in this troubled world than we know about. At times of reflection we can appreciate that although they come in different sizes, colours and varieties, just like people, they do not seem to vie with each other for supremacy, nor as far as we know do they show jealousies, they just seem to grow and give love and beauty to all who see them. They are with us on every occasion from birth until death, helping the tongue-tied to 'say it with flowers', contributing to medicine, healing and cooking.

I feel I have not answered adequately the question, 'What has it all achieved?' but on looking back to the wonderful people I have met, the interesting countries I have visited, the remarkable sights I have seen and the gardens I have enjoyed, I ask myself if all this happened to me because I went out that rainy day to talk about flowers to those war-weary women in Kent. If so, I am glad I did, for it led me to a wonderful life with flowers.

Index

188

Useful Addresses

Edward Bach Centre, Mount Vernon, Wallingford, Oxfordshire OX10 0PZ

National Association of Flower Arrangement Societies of Great Britain (NAFAS), 21a Denbigh Street, London SW1V 2HF. Tel 071 828 5145

National Gardens Scheme (England and Wales), Hatchlands Park, East Clandon, Guildford, Surrey GU4 7RT

National Gardens Scheme (Scotland), 31 Castle Terrace, Edinburgh EH1 2EL

National Trust, 36 Queen Anne's Gate, London SW1 9AS. Tel 071 222 9251

Royal Horticultural Society, 80 Vincent Square, London SW1P 2PB. Tel 071 834 4333

Royal National Rose Society, Chiswell Green Lane, Chiswell, St Albans, Herts AL2 3NR. Tel 0727 50461

Belgium: Belgian Flower Arrangement Society, Kortrijhsesteenweg 834, Ghent 9000

Canada: Toronto Garden Club, 777 Lawrence Avenue East, Toronto, Ontario M3C 1P2

France: National Society of Horticulture (floral art), 84 rue de Grenelle, 75007 Paris

Italy: I.I.D.F.A., P.O. Box 229, 18038, San Remo

New Zealand: Floral Art Society of New Zealand, Murphy's Road, Papatoetoe

United States: National Council of State Garden Clubs Inc, 4401 Magnolia Avenue, St Louis, Missouri

The Garden Club of America, 598 Madison Avenue, New York, N.Y. 10022